THE YORK RE
in the light of the Qu

Front cover: Original building of The Retreat, York, from the gardens.
FROM A PAINTING BY WILLIAM CAVE

William Tuke the Founder

The York Retreat was founded in 1792 by William Tuke, a Yorkshire Quaker, and opened in 1796. Originally intended mainly for the benefit of members of the Religious Society of Friends, it has in fact always served the community as a whole and pioneered the treatment of mental disorders with sympathy and understanding. Its establishment had a profound influence upon public opinion, resulting ultimately in fundamental reform of the laws relating to mental illness.

The York Retreat
in the light of
the Quaker Way

Moral Treatment Theory:
Humane Therapy or Mind Control?

by

Kathleen Anne Stewart

William Sessions Limited
York, England

© Kathleen Anne Stewart 1992

ISBN 1 85072 089 4

Printed in 10 on 11 point Plantin Typeface
by William Sessions Ltd.
The Ebor Press, York, England

Contents

Page

Foreword	ix
Acknowledgments	xi
Introduction	xiii

CHAPTER ONE: *The Historiographical Debate: Perspectives on Moral Treatment Theory and The York Retreat* — 1

Introduction to the Historiographical Debate — 1

Samuel Tuke, *Description of The Retreat* — 1

Gregory Zilboorg, *A History of Medical Psychology* — 9

Mary Glover, *The Retreat, York: An Early Experiment in the Treatment of Mental Illness* — 9

William K. and E. Margaret Sessions, *The Tukes of York* — 10

Michel Foucault, *Madness and Civilization* — 11

Andrew Scull, *Madhouses, Mad-doctors, Madmen* — 13

Fiona Godlee, 'Aspects of non-conformity: Quakers and the lunatic fringe' — 14

Anne Digby, *Madness, Morality, and Medicine* — 15

Conclusion — 18

CHAPTER TWO: *The York Retreat: Program, Practice, Queries* — 23

Description of The Retreat Archives — 23

Quaker Debate/Exclusion or Admission of Non-Quaker Patients — 24

Location, Travel, and Economic Concerns — 26

Staff — 28

Patients — 30

  Admission — 30

  Treatment — 34

    Privacy/Trust — 34

    Manipulation of The Retreat Treatment Policy — 34

Manner of Environment	35
Moral Treatment as Discomforting	37
Causes of Insanity	38
Symptoms of Insanity	41
Conclusion	43

CHAPTER THREE: *The Quaker Context: The Role of Quakerism in The Retreat Asylum Reform* 49

Introduction to Quaker History	49
PART ONE: The Beginnings of Quakerism: The Heroic Period	50
1650-1700: A Reactionary Phenomenon with Emphasis on Inner Discipline	50
Moral Treatment of 1790: A Reactionary Phenomenon with Emphasis on Inner Discipline	51
The Founder: George Fox and the Inner Light Experienced	52
The Founder: William Tuke and the Inner Light Experienced	52
The Founders: George Fox and William Tuke and the Inner Light Intellectualized	53
George Fox: Righteousness and Perfectibility	53
William Tuke: Righteousness and Perfectibility Through Practice	54
George Fox and William Tuke: Shared Beliefs, Different Social Climates	54
George Fox and William Tuke: Economic and Employment Disadvantages Made Positive	55
PART TWO: The Evolution of Quakerism, 1700-1800: Period of Conservatism, Organization, and Quietism	57
Quietism: A Rationalization of Earlier Beliefs	57
Meeting for Worship: The Center of the 18th-century Quaker Community	58
Elders and Overseers	59
18th-century Meeting and The Retreat: Models of the Family	60
Conclusion	62

CHAPTER FOUR: *Conclusion: Integration of Historiography, Archival Material, and the Evolution of Quakerism* 67

Afterword	72
Appendix	73
Bibliography	76

Illustrations and Tables

William Tuke, founder of The York Retreat	ii
Main entrance of The York Retreat	viii
Title page of Samuel Tuke's *Description of The Retreat 1813*	4
Samuel Tuke, the author of *The Description of The Retreat*	6
Superintendents and Visiting Medical Officers	16
'The Appendage', early 1800's	29
Katherine and George Jepson in silhouette	29
Title page of *Rules for the government of Attendants and Servants,* 1847	31
William Tuke's handwriting, 1792	47
George Fox, founder of Quakerism	48
William Tuke, founder of The York Retreat	48
Henry Tuke, eldest son of William Tuke	56
Friends Asylum, America's first psychiatric hospital	61
Yearly Meeting Epistle to Friends, 1783 signed by William Tuke, as Clerk	66
Issues and Perspectives of The York Retreat and Quakerism	68
Open-Air Treatment at The York Retreat, 1932	72
Pages from The York Retreat's Visitors' Book	74
Aerial view of The York Retreat, 1989	81

Unless otherwise indicated, all illustrations are by courtesy the Archives of William Sessions Limited

THE ORIGINAL BUILDING, MAIN ENTRANCE

Towards the town is a magnificent view of The Minster soaring up above the red roofs around it and the back of The Retreat looks across Walmgate Stray, which is open land for all time, while to the east lies York's new University, most beautifully landscaped to include trees, hilly rises, and a long curving lake.

Foreword

by Stuart C. Haywood, B.A., D.S.A., F.I.H.S.M.
Chairman of The Retreat Management Committee

THIS RE-EXAMINATION OF THE EARLY YEARS of the York Retreat is timely. It successfully challenges widely held critiques of moral treatment which inform views of contemporaries. It also provides a balanced view of the Quaker contribution to the care of the mentally ill, warts and all. The welcome conclusion is that the founders of The Retreat, on balance, deserved their reputation for breaking new ground.

The book is timely in another respect. It was in 1792, exactly 200 years ago, that York Quarterly Meeting approved William Tuke's detailed proposal for what became the 'Retreat of Persons afflicted with Disorders of the Mind'; to be followed in 1796 by The Retreat's establishment as a hospital for this purpose. So inevitably thoughts are now turning to The Retreat's place and role in the next 200 years.

Kathleen Stewart's book is therefore a welcome challenge to those charged with stewardship of the hospital and the adaption of its services to new circumstances. It is a reminder of how much has been achieved in the application of Quaker beliefs and values to the care of the mentally ill. The challenge for The Retreat is to continue to demonstrate the relevance of those beliefs and values into the next century.

Acknowledgments

SPECIAL APPRECIATION IS EXPRESSED to the Ford Foundation for making it possible for me to travel to The Retreat Archives at the Borthwick Institute of Historical Research in York, England. Gratitude is also extended to William and Margaret Sessions of York for their many courtesies, and to Dr Charles Cherry of Villanova University, and to Dr Jerry Frost of Swarthmore College for their enlightening consultations. I must thank Dr David Smith and the other archivists of the Borthwick Institute and my thesis advisor, Dr Anne Harrington, for their generous, thoughtful, and caring assistance. This paper clearly would not have been possible without Professor Harrington's personal and professional support. She has given my understanding of scholarship new meaning. On a personal note, I would like to thank my parents and grandparents for their combined guidance, understanding, and love, and Samuel Henderson Shuffler for his important and constant support.

Harvard University　　　　　　　　　　KATHLEEN ANNE STEWART
Cambridge, Massachusetts, USA
March, 1990

Note: With this publication of my senior thesis, written initially in partial fulfilment of the requirements for the Bachelor of Arts degree in History and Science at Harvard University, I want to express specific appreciation to Dr John Libertino of the Lahey Clinic in Burlington, Massachusetts and to Dr William Frist, Dr Richard Zaner, and Mark Fox of the Vanderbilt University School of Medicine in Nashville, Tennessee. Drs Libertino and Frist have been continually affirming of my desire to become a physician, and Dr Zaner and Mark Fox have been greatly encouraging of my interest in medical ethics. Words of thanks, too, are extended to Jeaneane Williams for her careful editorial assistance; to Peter Hunt for his caring support; and to William Sessions Ltd. and the staff at the Ebor Press for perceptive and sensitive guidance in the preparation of this manuscript for publication.

Vanderbilt University School of Medicine　　KATHLEEN ANNE STEWART
Nashville, Tennessee, USA
January 1992

Introduction

For many years, work on the history of psychiatry tended to reproduce . . . ideological self-images [of scientific and humanitarian progress] intact. Historians were all too prone to mistake intention for accomplishment, rhetoric for reality, and to draw a flattering portrait of gradual progress toward ever greater enlightenment. By the late 1960's, however, such interpretations were under sustained assault for their naïveté and inadequacies . . . the pendulum swung perhaps too violently to the opposite extreme, with the term reform now reinterpreted as the reverse of humane . . . a 'giant moral imprisonment . . .'.[1]

If ever a psychiatric institution was subjected to these extremes of historiographical analysis and reanalysis, it has been The York Retreat in England, founded in 1796 by the Quaker (Religious Society of Friends) reformist William Tuke. Historians such as Samuel Tuke, Gregory Zilboorg, Mary Glover, and William and Margaret Sessions have celebrated the humane methods of treatment employed by William Tuke and his followers. The progressivist image most closely associated with the work of Philippe Pinel in France – the chains removed from the mad as their essential humanity was realized – was also applicable in the English context. Under Tuke's reforms, the insane patient was no longer treated as a brute, but was instead recognized as a suffering soul. In the place of beatings, he received so-called 'moral treatment' that minimized external, physical coercion and emphasized kindness, gentleness, and sympathy.

More recently, however, in the wake of growing dissatisfaction with authoritarian science, there have been a series of radical attacks on this sort of Whiggish historical interpretation. Michel Foucault has argued that Tuke simply replaced the external forms of control with less overt and more dangerous and subtle internal forms of coercion. Andrew Scull believes that 'moral treatment' was not kindness for kindness' sake, but instead was a technology for reshaping deviant individuals into the 19th-century

---

[1] Andrew Scull, *Madhouses, Mad-Doctors, Madmen: The Social History of Psychiatry in the Victorian Era* (Philadelphia: The University of Pennsylvania Press, 1981), p.2.

xiii

bourgeois ideal of 'the productive citizen'. Fiona Godlee, elaborating on Scull's historiography, focuses on the irony that Quakers, who once had been religious nonconformists, became strict enforcers of conformity at The Retreat. Anne Digby's comprehensive study includes the observation that The Retreat's success relied on an ignominious system of rewards and punishments that reduced patients to the status of schoolchildren.

It is the thesis of this paper that these two extremes of interpretation – what one might call the 'madonna'/'whore' syndrome in the historiography of 19th-century asylum reform – in fact obscure much more than they illuminate. It will be argued here that we are dealing with a highly complex historical situation that was notable, above all, for its ambiguities and moral gray zones. The goal of this paper will be to break out of the dichotomizing straitjackets characterizing much of the historiography of this field. To that end, I will be setting my research in The Retreat archives at the Borthwick Institute of Historical Research in York, England in dialogue with both current and past historiographical interpretations of the development of 'moral treatment'. The central contribution of the paper will be its effort to re-examine the ideals of moral treatment in the context of the evolution of Quakerism, an aspect of the moral therapy story which has, to date, been neglected or only superficially examined by most other historians.

CHAPTER ONE

The Historiographical Debate: Perspectives on Moral Treatment Theory and The York Retreat

Introduction

Much has been written about The York Retreat since its beginning in 1796. At first historians were content to sing only praises of the revolutionary moral treatment methods practiced there. However, in the 1960's, Michel Foucault began to attack the techniques employed at the asylum. Other historians such as Andrew Scull quickly added their variations to Foucault's arguments calling the practices carried out a 'moral imprisonment. It was not until 1985 that a somewhat less polemical approach to understanding The Retreat would be undertaken by historian Anne Digby. Nowhere, however, have the differing perspectives on the development of The York Retreat been laid in careful juxtaposition so that the pattern of changing historiographic conceptions about the nature of moral treatment could be critically examined. This chapter will seek to do just that. In my discussion, Samuel Tuke's *Description of The Retreat*, published in 1813, will be given specific emphasis because the *Description* is credited with being the first full-length account of a mental institution anywhere, and the work was clearly the reason that The Retreat became so renowned in its day. The *Description* reviews the first two decades of the reform attempted at York; the archival documents I propose to examine span the identical time period.

Samuel Tuke, *Description of The Retreat*

Samuel Tuke, who was William Tuke's grandson, stated shortly after the appearance of his study that 'The great object of my publication was to furnish facts for those who were far better able than myself to employ them for the general good'.[1] Samuel intended his treatise to give practical information about The Retreat which would aid others in carrying out

1

similar efforts at reform. Tuke's *Description of The Retreat* received glowing reviews, and a particularly important one appeared in the *Edinburgh Review* in 1815.[2] Reverend Sydney Smith wrote:

> The great principle upon which it [The Retreat] appears to be conducted is that of kindness to the patients. . . . When a madman does not do what he is bid to do, the shortest method, to be sure is to knock him down . . . [or to use] straps and chains. . . . But the Society of Friends seems rather to consult the interest of the patient than the ease of his keeper; and to aim at the government of the insane, by creating in them the kindest disposition towards those who have the command over them.[3]

New institutions based on the *Description* were quickly proposed, a prominent example being the London Asylum initiated by Edward Wakefield.[4] A Parliamentary Committee to monitor most aspects of asylum management and patient treatment was begun in 1815 as a response to the public's reaction to Tuke's book.[5] The construction of a southern Retreat was also suggested.[6] In America, Tuke's *Description* had direct impact upon the founding of the Frankford (later Friends), McLean, Bloomingdale, and Hartford Asylums.[7] Tuke gave talks throughout Europe about the methods of The Retreat, and he traveled to France specifically to visit Pinel's Bicêtre. What had 'started as a local, private, sectarian experiment in charity wrought a fundamental change in the attitude to the insane in England and spread throughout the world'.[8]

What was the actual content of this significant work which was sold out three years after its publication?[9] Tuke begins his commentary by stating that The Retreat 'has demonstrated beyond all contradiction, the superior efficacy, both in respect of cure and security, of a mild system of treatment in all cases of mental disorder. . .'.[10] He states that 'guarded' care could protect Members from 'the indiscriminate mixture' found in the large public institutions.[11] According to Tuke, the purpose of The York Retreat was to protect Members of the Society from the non-Quaker patients and staff dominant at most other asylums, not to exclude non-Members from benefiting from The Retreat's care and philosophy. Anne Digby has argued that The Retreat sought to exclude non-Quakers until 1820, but the real practice in the first two decades of operation appears to have been a more subtle one. The Retreat probably functioned more from the standpoint of 'protectionism' than from 'exclusionism'. While the net effect may have been the same, non-Quakers were, in all likelihood, not restricted from admission but instead reluctant to enter such a separatist community.

Continuing on the issue of exclusionism versus non-exclusionism, Tuke quotes from an important meeting held in 1792: 'As the benefit of the proposed institution is intended to be extended to those who are not strictly Members of our Society, it is the judgement of this Meeting that subscriptions may also be received from such persons'.[12] However, he also emphasizes the fact that Quaker patients had previously experienced 'great loss . . . by being put under the care of those, who are not only strangers to our principles; but by whom they are frequently mixed with other patients who may indulge themselves in ill language and other exceptionable practices'.[13] Tuke here inadvertently reveals an early discrepancy in policy at The Retreat. The Retreat founders were willing to accept money from non-Members, but in the next breath they spoke of the ill effects of 'mixing' Quaker and non-Quaker patients. This quirk in attitude was surely not lost to non-Friends.

Tuke then writes of admissions procedures and the classification of patients. He states, for example, that

> Experience has this year abundantly convinced us, of the advantage to be derived from early attention to persons afflicted with disorders of the mind . . . encourage the friends of those . . . afflicted . . . to remove them early, and to place them under proper care and treatment.[14]

The Retreat was concerned from the beginning about the duration of insanity and its relation to curability.

Also, patients, once admitted, were classified according to social position. There were to be 'apartments in which patients with a servant may be accomodated [sic], without mixing with the other patients'. Furnishing in the patient rooms 'varies, according to the terms upon which the patient is admitted, and to his state of mind. . . . The beds of those who are not of the lowest class, are of better quality. . . .[15] . . . patients of the superior class occupy the dining room as a day room. The bedrooms of this class are in the attic of the centre building. . .'.[16]

Tuke continues by outlining the governance of the asylum. A committee was to be responsible for the 'immediate care and management of the undertaking' and, as a footnote, it was observed that 'The Committee appoints three female visitors, one of whom is changed every month'.[17] Tuke again inadvertently reveals a discrepancy between policy at The Retreat and Friends philosophy by referring to the female visitors only in a passing citation. Women were said to be treated as equals in Quakerism, but in reality they seem only to have been recognized as an afterthought. The admission of non-Members was left to the discretion of the all-male and all-Quaker committee.

What follows next is a description of the grounds and facilities at the asylum. Efforts in construction of The Retreat were made more for cure and comfort than for the often 'excessive attention to safety' that characterized the design of most other hospitals of the time.[18] 'Cast iron window frames were substituted for the bars which in other institutions kept out light.'[19]

DESCRIPTION

OF

THE RETREAT,

AN INSTITUTION NEAR YORK

For Insane Persons

OF THE

SOCIETY OF FRIENDS.

CONTAINING AN ACCOUNT OF ITS

ORIGIN AND PROGRESS,

The Modes of Treatment,

AND

A STATEMENT OF CASES,

By SAMUEL TUKE.

With an Elevation and Plans of the Building.

YORK:

PRINTED FOR W. ALEXANDER, AND SOLD BY HIM;

SOLD ALSO BY M. M. AND E. WEBB, BRISTOL:

AND BY DARTON, HARVEY, AND CO.; WILLIAM PHILLIPS; AND

W. DARTON, LONDON.

1813.

There were no cells, few restrictive barriers, and every effort was made to avoid appearing like a place of confinement.

The basic form and operation of The Retreat described, Tuke moves on to discuss the critical issues of medical and moral treatment. He alludes to the experiments of Dr Fowler, the first Retreat physician, in which

Bleeding, blisters, seatons, evacuants, and many other prescriptions, which have been highly recommended by writers on insanity, received an ample trial; but they appeared to the physician too inefficacious, to deserve the appelation [sic] of remedy . . . [and] a very strong argument against them arose, from the difficulty with which they were frequently administered; as well as from the impossibility of employing powerful medicines, in a long continuance, without doing some injury to the constitution. The physician plainly perceived how much was to be done by moral, and how little by any known medical means. He . . . directed . . . that any medicine he might prescribe by way of experiment should not be administered, where the aversion of the patient was great. . . .[20]

Concerning the theory and philosophy behind the medical and moral treatment, Tuke continues that, 'The inexplicable sympathy between body and mind, appears to exist in a morbid degree, in this description of persons . . . there is more connexion [sic] between sound mind and body than is generally imagined. . .'.[21] Quakers stressed the same mind/body unity in their medical treatment as they did in their own personal worship, rejecting the dominant Cartesian dichotomy between mind and body so widely accepted at the time. Chapter Three of this treatise, 'The Role of Quakerism in The Retreat Asylum Reform', gives a more detailed description of the parallels between Quaker beliefs and moral treatment.

On the practicalities of moral treatment, Tuke stresses the importance of 'insane patients being under the frequent observation of [and in conversation with][22] persons of knowledge, judgement and probity'.[23] This intimate interaction was an argument against sending Quakers to larger institutions where the number of patients was too substantial 'to come under proper inspection of the superintendent'.[24] Realizing that moral treatment was more effective for small patient groups, Tuke beat recent historians such as Fiona Godlee and Andrew Scull to their conclusion that 'when large pauper asylums tried to adopt the 'moral therapy', all 'humane and individualistic aspects disappeared, and emphasis was placed instead upon the latent strength of moral therapy as a socially acceptable mechanism of enforcing conformity'.[25]

Tuke states that 'Insane persons generally have control over their wayward propensities. Their intellectual, active, and moral powers are usually rather perverted than obliterated'.[26] He continues that it is possible to stimulate superior motives and that fear may be used 'as a means of

5

Samuel Tuke – author of The Description of The Retreat, *published 1813.*

promoting the cure of insanity by enabling the patient to control himself'.[27] Further, Tuke writes that the principle of fear is 'considered as of great importance in the management of patients . . . but it is not allowed to be excited beyond that degree which naturally arises from the necessary regulations of the family'.[28] Historians such as Gregory Zilboorg and William and Margaret Sessions neglected to address the fact that Retreat staff routinely relied on fear techniques for managing patients. The reformist radical historians are aware of this method, but they have tended to misunderstand its meaning. In stressing the use of fear to enhance the 'power of the patient to control the disorder', Tuke reflects the Quaker belief in the importance of inner discipline and control (cf. Chapter Three).

Tuke elaborates his feeling by stating that 'There is much analogy between the judicious treatment of children, and that of insane persons'.[29] Foucault seems to have seized upon this statement and skewed [distorted] it when he writes that patients were treated as children at The Retreat. Tuke's important word 'much' tells us that there was no necessary assumption that the patients were actually children or were to be treated as such. In evidence of this, we may note the following further comment by Samuel Tuke:

> Those who are unacquainted with the character of insane persons, are apt to converse with them in a childish, or, which is worse, a domineering manner . . . tendency of such treatment is to make him indifferent to those moral feelings, which, under judicious direction and encouragement, are found capable, in no small degree, to strengthen the power of self-restraint; and which render the resort to coercion . . . unnecessary.[30]

Tuke observes that coercion is considered only as a 'protecting and salutory [sic] restraint'.[31] In the most violent cases of mania it was thought that the patient should be kept in a gloomy room so as not to overexcite his senses with the stimulus of light or sound.[32] Patients were probably secluded because this was believed to be beneficial to the patient and because the isolation of a troublesome patient helped to keep things running smoothly at The Retreat. Sometimes it became necessary to 'supply the patient by force with a sufficient quantity of food, to support life'.[33] This process was accomplished by placing a small door lock key between the teeth and turning it to raise the mouth. Next, liquid food was introduced using a strong spoon.[34]

Tuke goes on to explain a system of censorship at The Retreat which was held to have the best interest of the patient in mind. He states that means of writing were sometimes withheld from a patient as 'it would only produce continual essays on his peculiar notions; and serve to fix his errors more completely in his mind. Such patients are, however, occasionally indulged, as it is found to give them temporary satisfaction'.[35]

Closely related to the circumstance of writing was the selection of books. Works of the imagination, Tuke said, are 'generally, for obvious reasons, to be avoided. . . . The various branches of the mathematics and the physical sciences furnish the most useful class of subjects on which to employ the minds of the insane; and they should, as much as possible be induced to pursue one subject steadily'.[36] Samuel Tuke then cites the example of a patient who at first found it difficult to go through the easiest math problem, but after persevering, began to find that his ability to fix his attention was improving.[37]

While favoring some control over materials for reading and writing, Tuke seems also to have been sensitive to the danger of granting an unrestrained authority of censorship even to those who headed a 'humane' Quaker institution. He quotes Montesquieu: 'Experience continually demonstrates, that men who possess power, are prone to abuse it: they are apt to go to the utmost limits. May it not be said that even the most virtuous require to be limited?'[38] It remains unclear, however, who was to impose 'limits' on the 'virtuous' – would it be the Tukes themselves?

Samuel Tuke concludes his work with a summary of patients and cases. He observes that 'from the opening of this Institution, in the year 1796, to the end of the year 1811, one hundred and forty-nine patients have been admitted'.[39] He writes that, in contrast to Bethlem Hospital, 'Very few of the cases admitted to The Retreat, have been, in their commencement, at all connected with religious impressions'.[40] It will be seen in Chapter Two of this work that, in fact, his claim is incorrect. Tuke may have written that few of the cases were *caused* by religious impressions because, at the time, Quakers were often labeled insane by non-Quakers as a strategy for invalidating the beliefs of the Society of Friends. Tuke also alleges that whereas intemperance was prevalent as a cause of insanity for patients in public institutions, at The Retreat it was only the cause of three admissions. However, the archives indicate that many cases at The Retreat were caused by alcoholic 'overindulgence' (cf. Chapter Two).

Another important patient categorization that Samuel Tuke notes is that in contrast to other institutions such as Bethlem Hospital, The Retreat did not guard against admission of old cases, and, in fact, 'a large majority of cases admitted into The Retreat, have not been recent'.[41] As will be seen, the archives again cast doubt on Tuke's claims. He represents that, 'As we . . . profess to do little more than assist Nature, in the performance of her own cure, the term *recovered*, is adopted in preference to that of cured'.[42] This terminology was perceptive because many patients were not 'cured' but only 'temporarily recovered', and they were returned to The Retreat many times. 'Recovered' was used to infer that 'the patient is fully competent to fulfill his duties, or is restored to the state he was in previous to the attack'.[43]

8

Gregory Zilboorg, *A History of Medical Psychology*

Gregory Zilboorg, in *A History of Medical Psychology* (1941), continues in the historiographic tradition forged by Samuel Tuke. Zilboorg describes William Tuke as an 'efficient and scientific reformer'.[44] He states that

> The automobile and the airplane have made more progress in forty-odd years of the 20th century than did the social consciousness of the physician between 1563, when Weyer published his *De Praestigiis Daemonum*, and 1792, when William Tuke started his plans for the foundation of a hospital for the mentally ill and Philippe Pinel, appointed physician in charge of Bicêtre, started removing the chains from the mentally ill.[45]

Zilboorg suggests that the 'old Greek ideal stressing the responsibility of the individual citizen to the State was gradually being replaced by the revolutionary ideal of the duty and responsibility of the State toward its citizens'.[46] Zilboorg makes no mention of the fact that The Retreat was founded by a group that was not at all in alliance with 'the State'. Quakers suffered considerable fines and losses at the hands of the British government, and the British state proffered no special responsibility toward its Quaker citizens. The Retreat grew out of a community that had felt, from its beginnings in the 1650's, a particular obligation to care for its individual Members. The evolution of the 'sense of Quaker community' and the responsibility of the Meeting for its Members will be more fully examined in Chapter Three.

Zilboorg cites the death of Hannah Mills as the immediate catalyst leading to the founding of The Retreat at York, and he writes that the institution 'was the beginning of a new era in the treatment of the mentally sick. Restraint and abuse were replaced by kindness and tolerance, by working in the garden and gentle exercise on the surrounding grounds, by light recreations and amusements'.[47] No mention is made of secluding rooms or the use of fear in treatment as previously discussed. Zilboorg observes further that 'William Tuke had amply demonstrated that mechanical restraint was seldom necessary, that kindly personal attention, outdoor exercise, and regular employment were much more conducive to rational behavior, and that the best form of restraint is self-restraint'.[48] Zilboorg, as a psychoanalytically-oriented psychiatrist, had a personal investment in describing The Retreat as a rosy, non-biological, humane form of treatment. By celebrating the methods used at The Retreat, Zilboorg validated his own psychoanalytic work which stressed a 'talking' cure rather than chemical intervention.

Mary Glover, *The Retreat, York: An Early Experiment in the Treatment of Mental Illness*

Mary R. Glover, former Fellow of St Hugh's College, Oxford and late Director of Social Studies at Keele University, follows in the tradition of

Zilboorg describing William Tuke and The York Retreat in her volume, *The Retreat, York: An Early Experiment in the Treatment of Mental Illness* (1984). Glover begins her analysis by recounting the terrible condition of treatment for the insane in the 18th century, a time in which 'the prevailing idea was that the mentally ill had become somehow sub-human and insensitive, that they were in fact a species of animal, filthy, comic, often dangerous'.[49] She fails to address the fact, however, that Quakers had never viewed the insane as animals and that George Fox called for the formation of a house for the insane well back in the 17th century. Quakers, indeed, always seemed to realize the 'humanness' of the madman, primarily because of the 'Inner Light of God' they believed to be present in each individual. Glover directs only about four superficial pages to Quakerism rather scantily noting the beliefs of Friends as regard for simplicity, pacifism, 'that of God' in every individual, and a refusal to take oaths.[50] She seems to have been unconcerned about the reasons Quakers waited for a century and a half after the forming of the Society of Friends to found an institution for the insane, conditions which are attended to directly in Chapter Three of this analysis.

Mary Glover does aptly describe the development of The Retreat at York with a solid account of the asylum's staff and with considerable detail afforded to the design and construction of the buildings. She writes of the 'loving attention' given to patients by George Jepson, the superintendent,[51] and observes that restraints were rarely used, though some of the women patients thought 'their green belt and wrist straps smart'.[52] Glover also records that the importance of food 'was fully recognized' and that it was a well-established fact that 'meals were ample and varied'.[53] Her account is, however, often idealized and ideological and, like Zilboorg, she fails to address the less pleasant issues of secluding rooms, heroic treatments, and the use of fear as a part of the cure.

Glover was a deeply religious person who created a lecture series on the Old and New Testaments at Keele University. She also served on the Chapel Committee there, and created a Sunday school for faculty children. Mary Glover lectured on 18th and 19th-century social developments while at Keele, and she became interested in the history of prison reform. Her analysis of The York Retreat appears to have been an extension of her work in penal reform as well as an indirect celebration of her religious beliefs.

William K. and E. Margaret Sessions, *The Tukes of York*

William and Margaret Sessions give a similarly glowing account of The Retreat in their book, *The Tukes of York* (1971). Like others, they accept the idea that the death of Hannah Mills was the chief impetus behind the founding of The Retreat[54] (but cf. Chapter Two). The Sessions describe The Retreat as having the appearance of a small farm where, 'potatoes were grown, their own cows supplied the family with milk and butter, and on the north side was a garden for fruit and vegetables, flowers and shrubs'.[55] The Sessions add, 'The siting of The Retreat was truly inspired, as today it still commands an open view all around from its slight eminence. Towards the town is the magnificent view of The Minster . . . the back of The Retreat looks across Walmgate Stray, which is open land for all time, while to the east lies York's new University. . .'.[56] The Sessions write of the beech trees planted by 'the father of the little family' which still line the front wall.[57] Like Zilboorg and Glover, however, the Sessions' report fails to address the less than perfect aspects of The Retreat.

Sessions Quaker printing firm, established in 1811, has printed The Retreat Reports since 1822 and still does so today. Mary Glover's book on The Retreat was also published by Sessions. William Haughton Sessions (1878-1966) was Hon Treasurer of The Retreat for 33 years (from 1930-1963), longer even than Samuel Tuke, and E. Margaret Sessions, his daughter-in-law, was Deputy Chairman of Governors for 15 years, so the Sessions of York have enjoyed and had a long and close connection with the dedicated work of The Retreat.

Michel Foucault, *Madness and Civilization*

By contrast, Michel Foucault is perhaps too readily aware of the limitations of The Retreat in his *Madness and Civilization* (1965). Foucault's goal in his groundbreaking work was to demythologize the image of The Retreat as 'that happy age when madness was finally recognized and treated according to a truth to which we had too long remained blind'.[58] Foucault begins by quoting from Charles Gaspard de la Rive who, after visiting The Retreat in 1798, had written a letter to the editors of the 'Bibliothèque Britannique' about this new establishment for the insane. De la Rive wrote:

> If the soul momentarily quails at the sight of that dread disease which seems created to humiliate human reason, it subsequently experiences gentler emotions when it considers all that an ingenious benevolence has been able to invent for its care and cure. The house is situated a mile from York, in the midst of a fertile and smiling countryside; it is not at all the idea of a prison that it suggests, but rather that of a large farm; it is surrounded by a great, walled garden. No bars, no grilles on the windows.[59]

Foucault states that images such as the above are based on 'imaginary forms: the patriarchal calm of Tuke's home, where the heart's passions and the mind's disorders slowly subside. . .'.[60] In reality, the legend of Tuke transmits 'mythical values' because 'beneath the myths themselves, there was an operation, or rather a series of organizations, which silently organized the world of the asylum, the methods of cure, and at the same time the concrete experience of madness'.[61] Foucault believes that Tuke's gesture has been regarded as a liberation when actually 'The Retreat served as an instrument of segregation: a moral and religious segregation which sought to reconstruct around madness a milieu as much as possible like that of the Community of Quakers'.[62]

Foucault continues: 'The religious and moral milieu was imposed from without, in such a way that madness was controlled, not cured'.[63] At The Retreat, religion 'does not attempt to preserve the sufferers from the profane presence of non-Quakers (as Samuel Tuke wrote in his *Description*), but to place the insane individual within a moral element where he will be in debate with himself and his surroundings: to constitute for him a milieu where, far from being protected, he will be kept in a perpetual anxiety, ceaselessly threatened by Law and Transgression'.[64]

In essence, Foucault suggests that scholars and others should re-evaluate the meanings assigned to Tuke's work. He feels that 'liberation of the insane, abolition of constraint, [and] constitution of a human milieu are only justifications. The real operations were different'.[65] Foucault argues that Tuke substituted for the 'free terror of madness the stifling anguish of responsibility'.[66] He states that at The Retreat 'madness is childhood. Everything at The Retreat is organized so that the insane are transformed into minors'.[67] Foucault seems to weaken his argument here by an apparent self-contradiction. He says that the patients were treated as children, but he then criticizes the fact that they were given what would seem to be the quintessentially 'adult' responsibility of self-control. Foucault presses ahead with the suggestion that the nature of occupational therapy at The Retreat be re-examined. He writes: 'In the asylum, work is deprived of any productive value; it is imposed only as a moral rule; a limitation of liberty. . .'.[68] Chapter Two of this analysis will examine the validity of his claim.

Foucault continues further that the 'partial suppression of physical constraint was part of a system . . . in which the patient's freedom, engaged by work and the observation of others, was ceaselessly threatened by the recognition of guilt'.[69] He observes that the

> science of mental disease, as it would develop in the asylum, would always be only of the order of observation and classification. It would not be a dialogue. It could not be that until psychoanalysis had exorcised this phenomenon of observation, essential to the 19th-century asylum, and substituted for its silent magic the powers of language.[70]

Foucault concludes his commentary saying: 'Closed upon these fictitional values, the asylum was protected from history and social evolution'.[71] Chapter Three of this presentation will argue that The Retreat was distinctly influenced by the evolution of Quakerism, raising doubts about the assumption that this or any institution can exist in a 'historical vacuum'. In addition, numerous visitors from all over the world came to The Retreat, once more pressing the validity of Foucault's perception that the asylum at York was 'protected from history and social evolution'. (See the Appendix for a transcription of the *First Visitors Book*.) Foucault argues that 'In fact, he [Tuke] isolated the social structure of the bourgeois family, reconstituted it symbolically in the asylum and set it adrift in history'.[72] Again, he seems to contradict himself when he postulates that The Retreat was above all a Quaker community, and then suggests that the institution sought to recreate the atmosphere of the bourgeois family. Jerry Frost, a leading Quaker historian and currently Professor of Religion at Swarthmore College, stated in an interview that Quakers could not possibly have constructed a bourgeois environment because such an ideal explicitly contradicts fundamental Quaker beliefs[73] (cf. Chapter Three).

Andrew Scull, *Madhouses, Mad-doctors, Madmen*

Andrew Scull, in *Madhouses, Mad-doctors, Madmen* (1981), writes that we 'go astray when we accept at face value what Tuke and his followers provide as an account of their activities'.[74] Scull states that it is incorrect for Tuke's 'admirers' to attribute Tuke's achievements to his 'superior moral sensibilities, while consigning their opponents to the status of moral lepers, men devoid of common decency and humanity'.[75] The practices at places like Bethlem – 'intimidation, threats, outright coercion'[76] – were not intemperate brutality, but a logical consequence of the world-view of the keepers which drew them to perceive that any madman was an animal.[77] In the 17th and through the 18th century, a lunatic's supposed insensitivity to 'heat or cold, hunger or pain, his refusal to abide clothing, and so forth were simply taken as confirmation of the correctness of the explanatory schema'.[78]

Scull argues that it was this world-view that Tuke and his followers were 'in the process of abandoning'.[79] The madman was no longer viewed as an animal, 'stripped of all remnants of humanity . . . he remained in essence a man, a man lacking in self-restraint and order, but a man for all that. Moreover, the qualities which he lacked might and must be restored to him, so that he could once more function as a sober, rational citizen . . . [an] image of bourgeois rationality'.[80] Because Scull sees a changing conception of insanity as the cause of Tuke's reform, he states that it is important to remember 'that conceptions of human nature do not change in a vacuum. They arise from a concrete basis in actual social relations . . . the ways men look at the world are conditioned by their activity in it'.[81] Scull observes that in the 17th century, society was dominated by 'subsistence forms of agriculture' and 'nature rather than man [was] the source of activity'.[82] When society shifted to manufacturing and competition in the workplace, there was a corresponding shift in awareness, a new sense that man could be a creator of his own environment. Men were thus 'taught to internalize . . .

new attitudes and responses, to discipline themselves'.[83] There developed a new 'faith in the capacity for human improvement through social and environmental manipulation. . .'.[84] In sum, 'just as hard work and self-discipline were the keys to the success of the urban bourgeoisie . . . so his [Tuke's] moral treatment propounded these same qualities as the means of reclaiming the insane'.[85] Scull concludes with the warning that moral treatment 'was no kindness for kindness' sake . . . moral treatment sought to transform the lunatic, to remodel him into something approximating the bourgeois ideal of the individual'.[86]

But Scull is perhaps unaware of evidence that the Quaker position on insanity was different from that of the rest of society, and had been so from the very beginning of the Friends movement in the 1650's. Historian Jerry Frost states that Quakers in the 17th century believed in the humanness of the madman, the capacity for human improvement, and in the possibility of the internalization of standards. Scull errs in claiming that patients were shaped into the bourgeois ideal of the individual because he forgets that Quakers were not members of the bourgeoisie and did not share its values. Although Quakers gained in economic and business standing in the early 19th century, they were not actually assimilated into 'bourgeois' culture. Friends remained 'outsiders' much in the same way that Jews of Western Europe did. In the 19th century many Jews gained in economic status, but they remained distinct and separate from the center of bourgeois society. Scull's discussion of a 'changing conception of insanity' and its social roots is an interesting but inaccurate analysis of the origins of The Retreat. An alternative explanation is suggested in Chapter Three of this essay.

Fiona Godlee, 'Aspects of non-conformity: Quakers and the lunatic fringe'

Fiona Godlee, in her article 'Aspects of non-conformity: Quakers and the lunatic fringe' (1985), begins by stating that 'The Retreat at York was above all a Quaker asylum, initially run by Quakers exclusively for Quaker patients'.[87] This baseline assumption will be critically examined in Chapter Two. Godlee writes that the irony of moral treatment was that when large pauper asylums attempted to adopt the 'moral therapy' model, all 'humane and individualistic aspects disappeared, and emphasis was placed instead upon the latent strength of moral therapy as a socially acceptable mechanism of enforcing conformity'.[88] Godlee sees that 'removing the necessity for the asylums' crudest features . . . made the reality of . . . imprisonment and control far more difficult to perceive'.[89] Efficacy in treatment and not humanity, says Godlee, seemed to 'hold sway' – reliance on non-medical therapies came not from the fact that the reigning medical approaches were inhumane, but that they were ineffective.[90] Godlee argues that Tuke advised the 'desire for self-esteem' rather than 'fear' not out of compassion, but because self-esteem operated 'more powerfully'.[91]

(However, as stated earlier, Samuel Tuke was quite open about 'fear' as a controlling technique.)

Godlee believes that for Tuke, 'Outward appearance was deemed more important than the state of inner being. This is the very antithesis of Quaker belief, a major focus of early Quaker protest having been empty religious observances associated with the established Church'.[92] Quakers who themselves had once used clothes as a form of protest now insisted that they control patients' dress. In addition, the staff was also preoccupied with social niceties (for example, behavior at tea parties).[93] Kindness was the most important aspect of moral treatment, but it was not the aim. Instead, the asylum keeper sought to achieve conformity through 'non-violent management . . . and to reclaim [the insane], if possible, for society'.[94] In essence, 'The Tukes and their colleagues developed techniques for encouraging conformity in the insane; while their Quaker forbears, as religious and social non-conformists, were persecuted and disqualified as madmen.'[95]

The alleged irony of the situation is highlighted through a brief outline of the history of the Quaker movement beginning in the north of England in the 1640's 'with the wanderings of an apprentice leather worker, George Fox'.[96] Quakers, 'with their challenge to institutionalized and dogmatic religion and their obstinate affirmation of social and sexual equality . . . struck at the heart of English social structure'.[97] When Friends began to stress reason in their worship as a result of growing hostility from the rest of society, they began to consider as well the broader effects of uncontrolled enthusiasm. There was a shift away from 'evangelicism . . . through discipline',[98] a change from a 'loosely structured charismatic movement to classical religious sect'.[99] Godlee writes as if she is surprising us with a radical conclusion. Yet, it seems clear that Quakerism was no different from other unstructured movements; it had to take on rules to survive. This consolidation of charisma into formulae was obviously reflected in practice at The Retreat (cf. Chapter Three).

Anne Digby, *Madness, Morality, and Medicine*

Anne Digby's comprehensive study of The York Retreat from 1796 to 1914, *Madness, Morality, and Medicine* (1985), begins with the statement that 'by the end of the 18th century the lunatic was beginning to be seen less as a brute than as human, heroic therapeutics inherited from classical times were being challenged by milder methods. . . . It was within this context of transitional theory and practice that The Retreat opened its doors in 1796'.[100] Like Scull, she states that the preception of madness had shifted from animality to irrationality.[101]

Digby writes that it was difficult to find 'suitable' staff for The Retreat and that there was a rapid turnover of employees. Tuke superintended for a

Superintendents

Timothy Maud	1796-1797	Dr Henry Yellowlees	1922-1929
George Jepson	1797-1823	Dr Neil MacLeod	1929-1938
Thomas Allis	1823-1841	Dr Arthur Pool	1938-1950
John Candler	1841-1846	Dr Alfred Torrie	1951-1956
Dr John Thurnam	1846-1849	Dr Cecil C. Beresford	1956-1962
Dr John Kitching	1849-1874	Dr John E. O'N.	
Dr Robert Baker	1874-1892	Gillespie	1962-1979
Dr Bedford Pierce	1892-1922	Dr Alistair M. Gordon	1979-

Visiting Medical Officers

Dr Fowler	1796-1801	Mr S. W. North	1878-1893
Dr T. Cappe	1801-1803	Dr Robert Baker	1892-1910
Dr W. Belcombe	1803-1826	Dr Bedford Pierce	1922-1932
Dr Caleb Williams	1824-1871	Dr Henry Yellowlees	1929-1932
Dr H. S. Belcombe	1826-1854	Dr Neil MacLeod	1938-1944
Dr D. Hack Tuke	1854-1860	Dr Arthur Pool	1950-1955
Mr W. D. Husband	1871-1880	Dr Cecil C. Beresford	1962-1966

full year before George Jepson assumed leadership. Dr Thomas Fowler, not a Quaker, was asked to serve as physician to The Retreat, and he did so from its opening until his death in 1801. At this point, Dr Cappe, also a non-Friend, took over as The Retreat physician.[102] Upon his death a year later, Dr Belcombe, again a non-Friend, became asylum physician. He would serve until 1826[103] when he was succeeded by his son who held this office until 1854. More than anything else, The Retreat practised a kind of lay therapy that was based on a common faith in God shared by staff and patients.[104] However, Digby herself raises questions about her own argument that the success of moral therapy relied on the shared values of staff and patients by demonstrating that the doctors were not Quaker and that there was clear difficulty finding suitable staff. On the other hand, it is unclear how involved the doctors were in practicing moral therapy, and whether or not they attended to other than the patients' physical ailments.

Digby then states that recovery was believed to occur as a result of 'divine rather than human will'.[105] The Retreat became a surrogate home and family to resocialize the patient. The asylum was constructed with a sense of 'practical humanity', in contrast to places like St Luke's where the mad were still living like animals in unheated, dirty conditions. The buildings and rooms were simple, yet clean and comfortable.[106] Activities included domestic chores and outdoor exercise. Female patients participated in sewing circles while the men chopped wood.[107] Digby writes that 'Convalescents were encouraged to find their way back into a wider social world: they were invited to visit the homes of local Quakers, to take tea at the York Quaker schools, and to attend First Day Meetings.'[108] The Retreat was 'intended as a kind home' and there were 'close ties of friendship and familial relationships'.[109]

Digby's most important argument focuses on the idea that patients were seen as schoolchildren to be re-educated with a strong emphasis on self-discipline.[110] The Retreat was in reality 'Janus-faced'. There was a tension between 'humanity towards the weak and the importance of encouraging self-discipline'.[111] There was a struggle in balancing external and internal restraint, a system of rewards and punishments, and viewing the patient as a minor.[112]

Anne Digby also writes that women staff at The Retreat were respected as much as men, an argument that Chapter Two of this paper will seek to qualify. She further observes that in 1818, there was a decision to begin admitting affluent non-Quakers into the institution for economic reasons (to support poor Quaker patients). According to Digby, the first non-Quaker patient was not actually admitted until 1820.[113] Thus, it was 'in defense of the charitable impulse that had been central to its original principles that The Retreat lost an even more fundamental attribute – its overall Quaker character'.[114] In 1796 most patients were of the 'poorer sort', but by the 19th century the institution had increasingly well-to-do patients.[115] Affluent non-Quakers, first admitted in 1820, were charged more to pay for poor Friends.[116] In this manner, The Retreat could 'subsidize a large proportion of its Quaker patients . . .' and provide them with treatment that otherwise would not have been available.[117] This paper will argue, in contrast, that many non-Quaker patients (Attenders, those married to Quakers, and those who had been 'disowned') were admitted prior to 1820, primarily to ensure filling all the available places. Non-Quaker patients were readily admitted when The Retreat was not full, an act clearly economically favorable to the asylum. Indeed, the very first patient admitted, Margaret Holt, was not a Quaker (cf. Chapter Two, p.25).

Digby's final account is of the patients. She notes that, 'while there is almost too much information on the objective world of the patient, evidence on their subjectively felt experience was often absent'.[118] Indeed, there was a most disappointing lack of diaries and personal letters from the patients, probably because, as mentioned earlier, writing was discouraged. The Retreat differed from most private mental institutions in the early 19th century because a majority of its patients were women (perhaps because women outnumbered men in the Society).[119] Also, subsidized treatment was available at The Retreat for the female 'non-breadwinner', and more female patients were paid for by subscription than men.[120] In addition, Digby writes that women were thought to be more susceptible to 'mental shipwreck' than men.[121] In terms of patient admissions, Digby notes that The Retreat's entrance policy was primarily 'social' and not 'medical'; i.e., the most important factor for admission was whether or not the applicant was Quaker, and the nature of the disorder was only secondarily considered.

Conclusion

The juxtaposition of the differing historiographical debates surrounding The York Retreat presents a spectrum of views ranging from the hagiographic to the frankly hostile. How is this to be explained? One useful distinction that can be made is that of the 'insider' versus 'outsider' ideology. Among the authors reviewed, some were standing inside The Retreat, identifying with its ideals, and earnestly attempting to explain them to the world. Others stood well beyond The Retreat in a milieu that seemed much less pretty, looked in through the windows, and sensed that The Retreat must somehow be made to belong to a wider community.

Samuel Tuke epitomized the 'insider' mentality. The Retreat was founded by his family, and he was an employee of the institution. His goal was to 'justify the ways' of William Tuke to man, not to probe critically and dissect. Although not a Quaker, Gregory Zilboorg also can be said to represent an 'insider' perspective on The Retreat. As a psychoanalyst who saw history converging on the work of Freud, the 'moral therapy' pioneered by The Retreat represented a 'force of Light and Humanity' intent upon beating back the darkness of crude medical intervention. Mary Glover's religious perspective was central to her work in penal reform, and she uncritically praised The Retreat by emphasizing the 'Christian' nature of moral treatment. It appears that Glover wished to show the advantage, if not the necessity, of combining reform with a Christian system of ethics. The Sessions, both established Quakers in the city of York, could be said to have a strong social investment in the affirmation of The Retreat and its story. Two members of their family had served on The Retreat's Board of Directors (see p. 11), and in a very real sense, it was their personal heritage and legacy they were engaged in exploring.

In contrast, Michel Foucault had no bonds to Quakerism, and, in fact, had never visited The York Retreat. Foucault criticized The Retreat as a part of his larger skepticism about any form of authoritarianism or religion. Andrew Scull, a sociologist, wrote about The Retreat in the context of his larger goal: uncovering the cultural agenda of psychiatry. Scull viewed The Retreat suspiciously, as suppressive and conformist in the treatment of the deviant individual. Fiona Godlee, a physician, may have represented The Retreat in a critical light because she felt it did not place enough emphasis on the importance of medical intervention. Anne Digby is not a Quaker and had no particular ties to The York Retreat. Her mind was undoubtedly open, but she was almost certainly limited by only a distant sense of familiarity with what it means to be a practicing Friend.

In the chapters of this treatise to follow, I will attempt to offer an historiographical interpretation of The Retreat's archives that draws upon the strengths of the perspectives of both the 'insider' and 'outsider'. My analysis will be 'insider' in that I am a sympathetic (if not uncritical) Member of the Religious Society of Friends, but also 'outsider' in that I have no investment in defending The York Retreat. I am not currently employed in the medical or psychiatric profession, and neither the community of York nor the Tuke family impact upon my personal or economic well-being. Chapter Two of this essay will offer a corrective historiographical interpretation of the first two decades of The Retreat's founding and operation, primarily to allow me to engage in a dialogue with the 'insider'/'outsider' historians who have explored the structure and philosophy of The Retreat. Chapter Three will seek to provide a detailed account of Quakerism during the first 150 years of the movement in order to offer a new perspective on the evolution of The Retreat and its development of moral treatment. Chapter Four will integrate a careful examination of the archives with the history and evolution of Quakerism in an attempt to understand how the structure of Quaker thought and practice might shed light upon some of the contradictions inherent in 'moral therapy' as a means for treating the 'troubled and insane'.

Notes

[1] Richard Hunter and Ida Macalpine, introduction to Samuel Tuke's *Description of The Retreat* (1813; rpt. London: Dawsons of Pall Mall, 1964), p.5.
[2] Richard Hunter and Ida Macalpine, pp.5 and 17.
[3] Richard Hunter and Ida Macalpine, p.5.
[4] Richard Hunter and Ida Macalpine, p.17.
[5] Richard Hunter and Ida Macalpine, p.19.
[6] Dr Charles L. Cherry, Professor of English and Associate Academic Vice President, Villanova University. Interview, July, 1989. Book on The York Retreat and Friends Hospital, *A Quiet Haven: Quakers, Moral Treatment and Asylum Reform* (Fairleigh Dickinson University Press, Rutherford, New Jersey, 1989).
[7] Richard Hunter and Ida Macalpine, p.19. In fact, the summers I spent working at Friends Hospital in Philadelphia first sparked my interest in learning about the Quakers' influence on asylum reform.
[8] Richard Hunter and Ida Macalpine, p.19.
[9] Samuel Tuke, *Description of The Retreat* (1813; rpt. London: Dawsons of Pall Mall, 1964), p.23.
[10] Samuel Tuke, p.vi.
[11] Samuel Tuke, pp.22-23.
[12] Samuel Tuke, p.31.
[13] Samuel Tuke, p.41.
[14] Samuel Tuke, p.59.
[15] Samuel Tuke, p.101.
[16] Samuel Tuke, p.103.
[17] Samuel Tuke, p.85.
[18] Samuel Tuke, pp.106-107.
[19] Samuel Tuke, p.105. These can still be seen today. I received a tour of The Retreat from Dr Alistair Gordon, current superintendent, in August, 1989.
[20] Samuel Tuke, pp.111-112.
[21] Samuel Tuke, p.116.
[22] Samuel Tuke, p.179.
[23] Samuel Tuke, p.117.
[24] Samuel Tuke, p.117.
[25] Fiona Godlee, 'Aspects of non-conformity: Quakers and the lunatic fringe' in *The Anatomy of Madness: Essays in the History of Psychiatry* (London: Tavistock Publishing, 1985) quotes Andrew Scull, pp. 73-74.
[26] Samuel Tuke, p.133.
[27] Samuel Tuke, p.149.
[28] Samuel Tuke, p.141.
[29] Samuel Tuke, p.150.
[30] Samuel Tuke, p.160.
[31] Samuel Tuke, p.163.
[32] Samuel Tuke, p.164.
[33] Samuel Tuke, p.169.
[34] Samuel Tuke, p.170.
[35] Samuel Tuke, pp.181-182.
[36] Samuel Tuke, p.183.

37 Samuel Tuke, p.185.
38 Samuel Tuke, p.189.
39 Samuel Tuke, p.207.
40 Samuel Tuke, p.208.
41 Samuel Tuke, pp.212-214.
42 Samuel Tuke, p.217.
43 Samuel Tuke, p.216.
44 Gregory Zilboorg, *A History of Medical Psychology* (New York: W. W. Norton & Company, 1941), p.292.
45 Gregory Zilboorg, p.315.
46 Gregory Zilboorg, p.315.
47 Gregory Zilboorg, p.572.
48 Gregory Zilboorg, p.579.
49 Mary Glover, *The Retreat, York: An Early Experiment in the Treatment of Mental Illness* (York: William Sessions Limited, 1984), p.4.
50 Mary Glover, pp.11-14.
51 Mary Glover, p.58.
52 Mary Glover, p.62.
53 Mary Glover, p.68.
54 William K. and E. Margaret Sessions, *The Tukes of York in the Seventeenth, Eighteenth and Nineteenth Centuries* (York: William Sessions Limited, The Ebor Press, 1971), p.58.
55 William and Margaret Sessions, p.62.
56 William and Margaret Sessions, pp.62-63.
57 William and Margaret Sessions, p.64.
58 Michel Foucault, *Madness and Civilization: A History of Insanity in the Age of Reason* (New York: Random House, 1988), p.241.
59 Michel Foucault, pp.241-242.
60 Michel Foucault, p.242.
61 Michel Foucault, p.243.
62 Michel Foucault, p.243.
63 Michel Foucault, p.245.
64 Michel Foucault, p.245.
65 Michel Foucault, p.245.
66 Michel Foucault, p.247.
67 Michel Foucault, p.252.
68 Michel Foucault, p.248.
69 Michel Foucault, p.250.
70 Michel Foucault, p.250.
71 Michel Foucault, p.253.
72 Michel Foucault, pp.254-255.
73 Jerry Frost, Professor of Religion, Swarthmore College. Interview, December, 1989.
74 Andrew Scull, *Madhouses, Mad-doctors, Madmen: The Social History of Psychiatry in the Victorian Era* (Philadelphia: The University of Pennsylvania Press, 1981), p.106.
75 Andrew Scull, p.106.
76 Andrew Scull, p.107.
77 Andrew Scull, pp.107-108.
78 Andrew Scull, p.109.
79 Andrew Scull, p.110.

[80] Andrew Scull, p.115.
[81] Andrew Scull, p.113.
[82] Andrew Scull, p.113.
[83] Andrew Scull, p.113.
[84] Andrew Scull, p.114.
[85] Andrew Scull, p.115.
[86] Andrew Scull, p.111.
[87] Fiona Godlee, 'Aspects of non-conformity: Quakers and the lunatic fringe' in *The Anatomy of Madness: Essays in the History of Psychiatry* (London: Tavistock Publishing, 1985), p.73.
[88] Fiona Godlee, pp.73-74.
[89] Fiona Godlee, quotes Andrew Scull, p.74.
[90] Fiona Godlee, p.75.
[91] Fiona Godlee, p.75.
[92] Fiona Godlee, p.75.
[93] Fiona Godlee, p.76.
[94] Fiona Godlee, p.76.
[95] Fiona Godlee, p.76.
[96] Fiona Godlee, p.77.
[97] Fiona Godlee, p.77.
[98] Fiona Godlee, p.81.
[99] Fiona Godlee, p.81.
[100] Anne Digby, *Madness, Morality and Medicine: A Study of The York Retreat, 1796-1914* (Cambridge: Cambridge University Press, 1985), p.1.
[101] Anne Digby, pp.2-7.
[102] Anne Digby, p.24.
[103] Anne Digby, p.24.
[104] Anne Digby, p.25.
[105] Anne Digby, p.26.
[106] Anne Digby, pp.37-42.
[107] Anne Digby, p.42.
[108] Anne Digby, p.45.
[109] Anne Digby, p.45.
[110] Anne Digby, p.60.
[111] Anne Digby, p.87.
[112] Anne Digby, pp.85-87.
[113] Anne Digby, p.102.
[114] Anne Digby, p.104.
[115] Anne Digby, p.180.
[116] Anne Digby, p.181.
[117] Anne Digby, p.181.
[118] Anne Digby, p.171.
[119] Anne Digby, p.175.
[120] Anne Digby, p.175.
[121] Anne Digby, p.175.

CHAPTER TWO

The York Retreat:
Program, Practice, Queries

THE ARCHIVES FOR THE YORK RETREAT, located at the Borthwick Institute of Historical Research in York, England, are remarkably well kept and complete. The archivists report that little has been discarded and that 'the voluminous correspondence – approximately 100,000 incoming letters – bears testimony to the careful preservation of the archives'.[1] In addition, The Retreat records include Directors' Minute Books, Visitors' Books, Subscription Books, General Ledgers, General Cash Books, Household Expenses, Patients' Disbursements, Building Accounts and Papers, Admissions Registers, Returns of Admission, Registers of Certificates, and Case Books. In this chapter, I will be concerned with examining the documents found in the archives beginning in 1792 when William Tuke first proposed The York Retreat, leading up to its actual founding in 1796, and continuing until 1812 – – the first two decades of The Retreat and its functioning under the direction of William Tuke. The use of these two decades also allows for an exact parallel of the time documented in Samuel Tuke's book, *Description of The Retreat*. The *Description* is the reference cited as the authoritative source on the creation and nature of The Retreat by historians such as Gregory Zilboorg, Mary Glover, Michel Foucault, Andrew Scull, and Fiona Godlee. The use of these two decades also defines a span for dialogue with writers and historians such as William and Margaret Sessions and Anne Digby, who themselves used the archives.

This chapter is not intended as a complete description of the practice of moral treatment at The Retreat. The archives from the first two decades are lacking in information that would make this sort of analysis possible. There are practically no records of how the patients themselves viewed their illnesses, or their treatment. One of the few references to the way in which a patient perceived himself was a curious phrase used by John Fawcett who described his condition as being like 'an egg without a yolk'.[2] In addition, the staff did not write about the nature of the moral treatment they practised. There are no in-depth descriptions of occupational therapy or of the exercise treatment thought to be so therapeutically beneficial. The methodology of this chapter will be to take the documents available in the archives and to reinterpret the evidence in order to engage in a historiographical dialogue with Samuel Tuke, Gregory Zilboorg, Mary Glover, William and Margaret Sessions, Michel Foucault, Andrew Scull, Fiona Godlee, and Anne Digby. The examination of the primary material will provide a window into many of the complexities and ambiguities that have not been previously incorporated into the dialogue regarding the moral treatment practised at The York Retreat.

The Quaker Debate

Among the initial documents found in The Retreat archives is a minute in the *Directors' Minute Book* which at first seems to support the claims of many of the exclusionist historians discussed in Chapter One:

> At a meeting of Friends held at York the 28th of the 6th Month, 1792, for the purpose of taking into consideration the propriety of providing a retired HABITATION, with the necessary advice, attendance, &. c. for the MEMBERS of our SOCIETY, and others in profession with us, who may be in a state of Lunacy, or so deranged in mind (not Idiots) as to require such a provision. Persons of this description (who are truly objects of great sympathy and compassion) are often from the peculiar treatment which they require, necessarily commited [*sic*] wholly to the government of People of other Societies, by which means the state of their own minds, and the feelings of their near connections, are rendered more dissatisfied and uncomfortable than would probably be the case if they were under the notice and care of those with whom they are connected in Religious Society. It appears therefore very desirable that an Institution should be formed, wholly under the government of Friends, for the relief and accomodation [*sic*] of Such Persons of all ranks with respect to property: This would doubtless, in some degree, alleviate the anxiety of the relatives, render the minds of the patients more easy in their lucid intervals, and consequently tend to facilitate and promote their recovery.[3]

This proposal continued by laying out seven distinct guidelines about the nature of The Retreat and its operation. First, physical conditions: there were to be ground and land purchased for 30 patients; the asylum was to be 'airy', near York, to have cows and a garden, and room for 'the Family' to exercise. Second, the asylum was to be established and supported by 'annuities, donations, and subscriptions' and would be promoted 'amongst Friends within the compass of this and other Quarterly Meetings'. Third, 'subscribers' would include those who donated £20. Fourth, donations of £100 from a Quarterly Meeting or £25 from an individual Friend before 1794, or a subscription of £50 for an annuity, entitled the person or Meeting responsible to 'nominate one Poor patient at a time on the lowest terms of admission'. Fifth, an Annuitant, Subscriber, or Donor of 'not less than two guineas in the first three years (being and continuing a Member of our Society) shall be a Member of the Meetings which are to be held for the government and superintendance [sic] of the Institution'. Sixth, fees would pay for 'board, medical advice, and medicines, and all other things necessary except clothing'. Costs would average 4 to 15 shillings per week, with expenses somewhat higher in particular cases. Board for servants would be 6 shillings per week, and admittance of servants must be approved in each case by the community. Lastly, fees for those from outside Yorkshire would be 8 shillings per week unless 'priveleged [sic] agreeable to number 4'.[4] (See number four of the seven guidelines listed above.)

Almost as an aside, scribbled at the top of the page, it was written that Hannah Mills, Friend from Leeds, died at the York Asylum on the 30th of the 4th month, 1790.[5] No other mention of this figure, mythically omnipotent in the accounts of The Retreat's founding written by Tuke, Zilboorg, the Sessions, Glover, and Digby occurs in the archival material for this period. The death of Hannah Mills might well have been the critical event needed to push William Tuke into action, but the actual founding of The Retreat was the product of a more complex historical, economic, and social situation (cf. Chapter Three).

William Tuke 'desired' that approximately 1,000 copies of the proposal outlined above be circulated among Friends in order to gain financial support for The Retreat.[6] In 1792, Lindley Murray was the largest donor, and there were six women on the list of 20 who gave money to support The Retreat.[7] Friends recognized the importance of fund raising to the viability of their institution because there was no support from the state for Quaker individuals. This information raises doubts about Zilboorg's argument that The Retreat was a reflection of State interest in the destitute (cf. Chapter One).

Returning to the Quaker versus non-Quaker admission debate, on the '27th of the 9th month, 1792', it was suggested that The Retreat accept patients who were 'not strictly Members of our Society' and take subscriptions from them as well.[8] In 1796 it was stated that 'Non-Friends must pay regular rate, but may be admitted'.[9] Indeed, the first application for The Retreat was for a Margaret Holt, 'wife of William Holt but she not herself a Member of the Society; the Committee proposed that she be admitted at 8 shillings a week, paying one quarter in advance'.[10] In 1797, George Jepson arrived as superintendent. He repeated 'that non-Quakers may be admitted, but not at reduced rates'.[11] In addition, in 1798, a special brochure was sent out which reiterated that the institution was not strictly for those who were 'Members of the Society' but that such patients who weren't must pay the regular price and were not 'to be indiscriminately admitted'.[12]

There are numerous examples of the admission of non-Quaker patients in the archives. A John Young ('not a Member of our Society but has attended our meetings and his wife is a member') was admitted in 1798 at 8 shillings per week.[13] Up to this point, four non-Quakers had been admitted to The Retreat. Thomas Wellington, having 'attended meetings for many years with his wife being a Member of the Society', was admitted as the fifth non-Quaker patient through a Special Meeting of the Committee on the 3rd of the 5th month, 1799.[14] A Joseph Lupton came the 20th of the 4th month, 1800, in low circumstances, 'but not being in Membership he is admitted at 8 shillings per week'.[15] On the 23rd of the 6th month, 1800, the Committee recorded 'three patients admitted last month including George Staniland not in Membership'.[16] On the 2nd of the 5th month, 1802, there was a special meeting held for the 'application of Elizabeth Smith of Whitby, who is not in membership but from representation of her situation such as within the intention of this Institution . . . agreed to admit her. . .'.[17] Joseph Collier, who 'has been a Member but is disowned', was admitted at 8 shillings per week, 'his being in low circumstances'.[18]

These records offer a striking refutation of Anne Digby's claim that non-Quaker patients entered only in 1820, and suggest that her argument about the success of The Retreat relying almost solely upon the shared religious values of staff and patients was not uniformly valid. In fact, many of the non-Quaker patients at The Retreat had originally been Quaker and had been disowned or 'read out of the Meeting' because they did not follow Quaker rules nor fully share the values of the Friends community. Quakers who did not conform to the rules of the Society were more than infrequently labeled as 'mad', and it at first appears that those who deviated from the 'norms' of Quakerism entered The Retreat only to be retrained in 'Quaker values' – the conformity of which Godlee, Scull, and Foucault write. In actuality, the archives demonstrate that the situation was considerably more complex. The reconciliation of the Quaker belief – respect for the individual because of the Inner Light – is juxtaposed with the need for following structured rules and is discussed through the Quaker belief in the value of a cultivated inner discipline (cf. Chapter Three).

Location, Travel, and Economic Concerns

In addition to the debate over whether or not to admit non-Quaker patients, other disagreements and concerns arose even before The Retreat was founded. Letters to William Tuke from Friends in 1793 revealed mixed responses. On the one hand, Thomas Woodruffe Smith wrote that 'My father in Law [sic] handed me a printed paper proposing the Establishment of a House for the Reception of Insane Persons of our Society near York. . . . An institution of this kind appears so desirable that I contribute 20 Guineas towards its establishment. . . . Distance from friends, the healthiness of the situation, the reasonable price of the necessities of life render it extremely probable'. On the other hand, Joseph Hadwell, writing from Liverpool, stated that there were 'several strong objections in the minds of Friends . . . 1) not sufficiently centric, considerable expense to convey patient generally in such a state as to require two men to conduct him there in a post chaise and 2) Poor Friends pay more if not from Yorkshire unless privileged agreeable to your proposal'. A W. Grover expressed concern about the location (London would be more central), and he suggested it be left up to subscribers to decide. He also felt that the terms for non-subscribing patients were too high and that Yorkshire had exclusive privileges it ought not to have.[19] Despite the reaction of some that the location should be more central, it was decided that in York the land prices were lower, the air was free of smoke, and the 'provisions would be cheaper because the area was fruitful for its population'.[20]

Concerns about location and the expense of travel and treatment actually proved themselves reasonably justified once The Retreat was under way and running. Finances often appeared as a great concern in letters. Although patients paid their fees based upon an innovative sliding scale system (the poorest Quaker patients paid 4 shillings per week and the poorest non-Quaker patients, 8),[21] payment was still a major difficulty for many families. The most extreme and worthy cases were sponsored by Meetings or benevolent individuals. One letter on such an individual lamented the fact that the family could not do more: 'I know not a family that would be more desirous of contributing for his [the patient's] support, but they are not in sufficient circumstances, to render him any pecuniary assistance'.[22] Another letter from a family member was more positive: 'If it is proper thou mayest tell Mary that . . . if she still grieves about the expenses she is putting me to, thou mayst [sic] say that I consider that is a trifling Point of View as I can cheerfully and comfortably pay the whole of it and hope she will give herself no uneasiness about that. . . '.[23]

Not only patients but The Retreat as well shared in the financial burden of care. In 1801, The Retreat was still soliciting money because the 'Debt with which it is still incumbered [sic] continues to claim the assistance of those who feel for the afflictions of their fellow creatures. The Retreat is not able to bring the yearly expenses of the Family within income from patients as yet'.[24] In 1802, the yearly income from patients was less than expenses by £13.[25] Records of the financial losses of The Retreat continue throughout the first two decades.

Travel was also an especially important topic of concern. Because The Retreat was located in the north of England, still rough country in the early 1800's, journeys there were long, hard, and expensive. Costs often included hiring someone to travel with the patient. The application for Hannah Burnham stated that 'she has had intervals of insanity for several years and also [is] in [a] state of bodily weakness and although present paroxysm commenced only 6 months ago. . . . Committee doesn't think eligible to admit her . . . the removal to so great a distance, in case of a temporary recovery'.[26] Another person wrote of her sister Mary, 'We think taking her from The Retreat a matter of importance as it would be attended with considerable difficulty and expense to get her returned there in case of a return of her complaint'.[27] Mary Young asked if 'Mother may be permitted a month longer . . . unsafe for so aged a person to undertake a long journey in a severe and cold winter'.[28] Tabatha Middleton wrote, 'The property of M. Bayes we apprehend will not exceed £100 after the expenses of her journey to York are defrayed'.[29] Not previously documented in the secondary literature, this and similar commentaries point to the conclusion that the cost of travel and treatment at The Retreat was frequently paid, at least in part, by selling the property of patients.

There were, however, also benefits to travel. Relatives who might not otherwise have accompanied patients came with them to The Retreat. Richard Dearman wrote 'an inlaw [sic] and a neighbor comes along with her whom I have no doubt will take the necessary care of her on the Road and will be able to describe her situation to thee more accurately than I can do it in writing. They have a few lines with them from a medical person in the neighborhood'.[30]

Staff

Staff were brought to The Retreat on what was for the time a unique 'trial' program. It allowed William Tuke and the other members of the Committee the time to decide if an employee was 'satisfactory'.[31] Tuke writes, 'Our staff should cherish in our patients the strengthening and consolitory [sic] principles of Religion and Virtue and aid solid reflection which leads to substantial peace and comfort'.[32] There seems, however, to have been difficulty in finding and keeping suitable staff. In one year, for example, Jane King left her position as housekeeper and Jane Wood, the cook, also left, and an inquiry was being made for a chambermaid.[33] One clear limitation on the employment pool was undoubtedly the fact that Tuke preferred employing staff from the Quaker community, and there were not enough Friends available for such specialized labor.

Heavy demand on staff is also likely to have been one of the reasons there was such difficulty in keeping employees. Tuke wanted the staff to dedicate even the majority of their private time to The Retreat. Staff lived at The Retreat, and they were thought of as an integral part of 'The Family'. The dismissal of married staff indicates that William Tuke thought such individuals would not be able to dedicate sufficient time to The Retreat family. It was stated that 'John Beall being lately married, it is thought proper for him to leave his place in the Institution as it does not suit him to

'The Appendage', *outside Walmgate Bar, early 1800's.*
COURTESY OF YORK CITY ART GALLERY

Katherine Jepson (née Allen)
(Matron and 'Female Superintendent'
1796-1823)

George Jepson
(Superintendent 1797-1823)

lodge in the house. . .'.[34] Tuke also wrote that Thomas Ventress and Jane Witherald were to marry, and an inquiry for others to take their places was being made.[35] In contrast, a marital state was prized in superintendents where a 'father and mother' image was promoted.

This brings us to the place of women at The Retreat, and the record is relatively encouraging. Anne Digby's claim that women were treated as equals, however, needs some qualifying. Women were an integral part of the staff at The York Retreat, and they were treated as equal to men at least in terms of their pay for superintending. In 1797, George Jepson came as superintendent for £50 a year.[36] When he married Katherine Allen, who had been appointed the previous year and became Housekeeper, which was the senior post for women, their joint annual salary was made £100. Like the Jepsons, Joseph and Mary Awmack served as the 'father and mother' superintendents of the Appendage, a building for convalescent patients sited near The Retreat.[38] Also, women were sometimes present at Committee meetings.[39] In addition, they were appointed as 'Visitors' to The Retreat. On the 25th of the 7th month, 1796, 'The Committee apprehending a benefit would arise from some women Friends visiting the House occasionally but not seldomer than once a week . . . it is agreed that three women be requested to perform this service, one of them to go out every month, and another to be chosen in her stead. The following are requested at present – Anne Tuke, Elizabeth Mason, Ann North'.[40] In the first two decades, the Female Visitors appear to have been more of a formality than a truly recognized part of the institution. There are no records of their having taken part in decisions about governing The Retreat, and their suggestions were only passed if they were approved by the exclusively male Committee. The Female Visitors, however, seem to have been active for the economic rights of women staff. At one meeting, it is recorded that they suggested that a present be made to Hannah Hall in recognition of her 'faithful services'.[41] The Committee further reported on the 29th of the 7th month, 1807, that 'upon the suggestion of the female visitors it has been agreed to raise the wages of Hannah Ponsonby to 12 guineas per annum to commence for the present year'.[42]

Patients

Admission

It was declared that, 'On the admission of Patients, the Committee should, in general, require a certificate, signed by a medical person, to the following: "I do hereby certify, that A B of C, aged .... years, is in a state of Insanity, and proper to be received into a house provided for the relief of persons of that description" '.[43] The fact that The Retreat wanted a certificate from a medical person suggests that moral therapy may have been less isolated from medical thinking than has often been claimed by

RULES

FOR THE GOVERNMENT

OF THE

ATTENDANTS AND SERVANTS,

AT THE

RETREAT, NEAR YORK;

WITH

INSTRUCTIONS

AS TO THE

MANAGEMENT OF THE PATIENTS, &c.

1847.

YORK :
PRINTED BY JOHN LEWIS LINNEY,
LOW OUSEGATE.
—
1847.

Title page of Rules for the government of the Attendants and Servants, 1847

Extract from the Rule Book showing a typical rule for the The York Retreat employees

65.—*Domestic and other Servants.*—All the house-servants, and others employed on the premises, are expected to set an example of order, quietness, kindness to the patients, and general good conduct; and to take care, in their intercourse with the patients, that the rules of the institution, and wishes of the superintendent, be strictly complied with.

N.B.—The copy of these instructions, which the several attendants and servants will receive on entering upon office, and which, it is expected, they will frequently peruse, is to be returned, with the keys and other articles under their care, in case of leaving the Institution.

historians. One function of the medical examination, though, may have been to rule out inappropriate cases with specifically identifiable organic roots. On the 8th of the 8th month, 1796, Joseph Reynolds' certificate demonstrated 'to The Retreat Physician and the Family, that his case is not insanity, but Epileptic Fits. . . . he is not a proper subject for this Institution – can't be kept more than a Quarter of a year; if Father prefers it he may be taken home'.[44]

In addition, it was written that it was

> desirable that some account should be sent, how long the patient has been disordered; whether any, or what sort of medical means have been used; and whether any disposition has appeared in the Patient to injure him or herself, or any other person; with any other treatment. Send applications for patients to William Tuke.[45]

The Retreat staff clearly wanted patient histories, and they were concerned from the beginning of The Retreat's operation about the connection between the length of the disorder and the probability of a cure. The philosophy seems to have been: the earlier the intervention, the higher the chances for successful treatment. The Retreat was quick to act on the imperative of this perspective. Rule 21 from 1799 declared:

> Experience demonstrates patients should be removed from their connections early and placed under proper care and treatment promptly to aid in cure . . . as an additional inducement to persons in strained circumstances, to adopt this salutory [sic] measure, it is concluded, that, in derangements not exceeding six months from their first appearance, those Members of our Society whose circumstances, in case of continuance, who would not conveniently admit of their paying more than eight shillings a week shall be entitled to an abatement of four shillings for one year, if not sooner recovered. Those Patients who, by the former Rule, would have been rated at four shillings per week, will, under this regulation be admitted gratis for a Year, if necessary.[46]

Eventually, the 'recentness' of the onset of disorder became the most important criteria for admission to The Retreat. In 1800, it was written, 'Two patients, whose disorder was recent, and who formerly would have paid four shillings weekly were admitted gratis, in consequence of the agreement entered last year. They are both recovered and discharged'.[47] Early intervention appears to have been the key to the cure. On the other hand, an application for Mary Richards, 'for many years afflicted by epileptic fits and . . . now insane', was refused because 'until there is more room, it is desirable to give a preference to recent cases, which probably admit of recovery'.[48]

Anne Digby has argued that admission was 'social not medical'. That is, Digby stated that the most important criterion for admission was whether or not the applicant was a Member of the Society of Friends. Abundant archival documents suggest that in fact, however, the staff was more conerned with the probability of cure (which they believed was associated with a brief duration of illness) than with whether or not the patient was Quaker or non-Quaker. Many Members as well as non-Members were refused admission because they were thought to be 'incurable'. The archives also qualify Samuel Tuke's claim that The Retreat did not turn away 'old' or 'incurable' cases. Tuke's assumption does hold true for the first few years when The Retreat needed patients for financial support, but when the 'house' was full even potentially lucrative cases of 'incurables' were turned away.[49]

This emphasis on curability needs to be seen within the larger context of increasing competition for admission to The Retreat. By the 26th of the 9th month, 1798, an additional building was proposed for patients as the 'house is so far filled as to render it probable more room will soon be wanted'.[50] In 1809, the Committee started to consider a facility 'for those needing least supervision' and purchased the land for the Appendage in 1810. This may have been the first 'half-way house'. Because of the emphasis on curability, families often attempted to wheedle by saying how patients would not be harmful to self or others, would not require too much work, or might even be useful to The Retreat. One John Southam wrote:

> he [the proposed patient] is I believe about 50 or 60 years of age, has been deranged in his intellects about 3 years, he was one year in Luke's Hospital from whence he was discharged uncured . . . is very quiet in his behaviour [sic] and pretty easily managed . . . has never attempted to do any hurt to himself or others and I do not know that coercion has ever been thought necessary.[51]

There were consistently more women admitted to The Retreat than men, probably because of the innovative program which allowed for subsidized stays for the needy. Men were more often breadwinners, and they were expected to pay their own fees. It is also possible that the founders accounted for the asymmetry of gender in admissions in terms of women's alleged greater susceptibility to mental illness – a product of the supposed instability associated with the female reproductive system.[52] At the same time, there were more applications for men than the founders had anticipated. It was written in 1799 that 'The Number of Male Patients having proved greater than expected, an additional building has been undertaken, and is nearly completed; and also a separate piece of ground walled in for their accommodation'.[53]

Treatment

PRIVACY AND TRUST

Privacy and trust were an important part of the moral treatment practiced at The Retreat. Letters, often the only source of information families had about their relatives, were extremely personal. They were written as if to a family member or close friend. Many letters to William Tuke were addressed to 'Esteemed Friend'.[54] One of the major duties of the superintendent must have been to take the time to answer the numerous letters from families. The phrase 'If thee think proper' is repeated over and over again in the correspondence. One letter concluded: 'If it is proper thou mayest tell Mary that we feel much affection and sympathy for her. . . .'.[55] Another wrote, 'If thou think proper please to hand Mary the few lines I had write [sic] on the other side. I don't wish to force it unless thou approve of it'.[56] Part of the stationery was torn away so it can be inferred that Tuke gave the patient the letter.

The importance of trust and privacy was also demonstrated in the actual therapy at The Retreat. The committee suggested a separate place with high walls be built in which the men could exercise in privacy.[57] The 'men's room was enlarged and a row of iron palisades was to be placed on each side of the walk from South front door to bath to separate men and women patients'.[58] The wall in the women's Yard was to be raised 'being [now] so low [as] to expose patients'.[59]

MANIPULATION OF RETREAT TREATMENT POLICY

The Retreat's system of mutual trust and respect seems to have been subject to manipulation by some patients and relatives. Despite the fact that families often asked about a patient's well-being, it appears that they frequently did not want them to come home. Many individuals stayed at The Retreat months after getting better. Samuel Botham wrote about John Summerland, 'I fear his reception at home would be such as would render him very liable to a return of his complaint, the consequences of which would be much dreaded'.[60] John Gibbins wrote of one patient,

> . . . we have no situation at the Present in View that would be suitable for her if she was to return at the end of the Quarter she must go to her mothers [sic] at Stourbridge and I believe my Mother would be quite afraid to have her Home just at Present and if she should return before she is quite well and have a relapse and be obliged to be sent again it will be an additional expense that my Mother's circumstances is not well able to base. If she could be allowed to stay another Quarter her Friends would be better satisfied of her recovery if nothing to the contrary should appear before that time is expired and there would be a little time to look out for a proper place for her. . . .[61]

The Retreat, by all appearances, respected the rights of its patients and perhaps was even somewhat overly indulgent of individual wishes. This practice at least casts doubt on the historiographical writers like Scull who lay stress on The Retreat's social function as one of conformity in cahoots with the larger society.

In addition to nurture and therapy, The Retreat often took on the burden of social work by placing patients within the community after release. It is recorded on the 27th of the 6th month, 1803 that 'As it sometimes may happen to be an accomodation [*sic*] to the patients on their recovery to be taken in to this or other Families as servants, but as such must always be considered liable to relapse, it appears to this committee reasonable that the monthly meetings to which such patients belong should indemnify this monthly meeting from any expense which may accrue on account of insanity'.[62] The Retreat staff was concerned with job placement for former patients, but they did not want the liability if something went wrong. Networks among the Friends community allowed for trial placement of patients away from the institution before sending them home. James Jermyn spent 'a few weeks at a Friends House . . . not sufficient to be returned home'.[63] Sometimes the staff employed former patients at The Retreat itself. For example, 'Abigail Tennant [was] to be chambermaid when discharged as a patient'.[64]

Foucault has argued that the treatment at The Retreat was aimed at controlling the patient's behavior through guilt, but the records indicate that life at The Retreat was hardly the subtle nightmare he envisions. A goodly number of patients seem to have been content to stay on as guests in 'The Family' even when they were no longer considered disordered. It was recorded on the 14th of the 4th month, 1797, that 'Ann Barrow also recovered, of which Friends informed but do not wish to have removed and she also appearing easy in her situation and useful to the Family, it is not thought necessary to urge her return till she or her Friends incline for it'.[65] Another place was proposed and 'it is left to her consideration whether to go there or remain in this House, which does not seem unsuitable, considering her peculiar state and probability of relapsing'.[66]

MANNER OF ENVIRONMENT

The physical surroundings at The Retreat were perhaps extravagant and indulgent, with grounds and buildings reminiscent of an affluent country club. Documents from 1794 demonstrate that the exceptional efforts of The Retreat staff went beyond 'studiously [avoiding] that gloomy appearance, which frequently occupies places appropriated for those who are afflicted with disorders of the mind'.[67] It is recorded:

> Wm Tuke Bo^t of John George Telford over 200 trees including 100 Beeches, 30 Black Italian Poplars, 50 Lombardy Poplars, 25 Oakes [*sic*], 25 Larches, 3 Cluster Pines, 2 Sugar Maples, 4 Berrybearing

Alders, 6 Silver Firs, 2 Tea Buckthorn, 4 White Berried Spindle Trees, 2 Hickory Nut, 6 Weymouth Pines, 4 Red Berried Spindle Trees . . . 3 pounds, 4 shillings, 9 pence [and] Wm Tuke Bo^t of Thomas Rigg [flowers, bushes, trees] including, 100 green hollies, 100 very large Quickwood, another 100 green hollies, 10 Mountain Ash, 10 Areatheophrasti, 2 Weeping Birch, 2 Red Virginia Cedars, 2 Horse Chestnuts, 2 American Spruce, 2 Oriental Platines, 2 Occidentals, 50 White Poplars, 50 Balsam, 2 Double Flowering Thorns, 2 Althea Frutex, 6 Red Barberry, 2 Long Bowing Honeysuckles, 2 Portugal Laurels, 4 Guilder Roses, 25 Tall Beech, 30 Scotch Firs . . . for 11 pounds, 6 shillings, and 1 pence.[68]

Not only were the grounds lavish and appealing, but interior decorating was exceptionally opulent; purchase orders for the 1790's read:

Large Oak Dressing Chest Drawers, Mahogany Square Table, 3 Pewter dishes and 5 plates, wire grate for a fireplace, 2 blankets, 10 chairs mahogany armed [69] [as well as] a mattras [sic], night stool, drising [sic] table, flat irons, fire irons, long glass, 2 basin stands, butters tray[70] and 6 ivory combs, 6 horn combs, 6 horn spoons, 2 drinking horns.[71]

Patients were also well supplied with food and drink. Alcohol was bought in large quantities for The Retreat family as indicated by this receipt:

Bo^t of Harrison & Co Dealers in Foreign Wines, Spiritous Liquors and Cordials of All Kinds [in 1808]: 1 kilderkin porter, 2 dozen Do, 24 bottles, 1 six gallon cask, 1 kilderkin porter, 1 bottle French Brandy, 1 Bottle Wine, 1 bottle Holl Gin, 1 Bottle Jamaica Rum, 4 Bottles Jamaica Rum, 2 Gallons Red Port, 9 bottles Red Port, 1 Kilderkin Porter for 8 pounds, 6 shillings, and 3 pence.[72]

This record is of special interest because a number of the patients were described as 'imbibing too much', and yet the archives indicate that The Retreat supplied its patients with generous amounts of alcohol. For many Friends of the time there was a moral standard against drinking, but inside The Retreat it was apparently thought that at least some patients were easier to handle when under the influence of a depressant.

A patient brochure documents how a general emphasis on comfort mingled with clear elitism at The Retreat. It stated that there were apartments 'in which patients with a Servant may be accomodated [sic], without mixing with the others'.[73] The Committee wrote:

There being a deficiency of accomodation [sic] for the superior female patients owing to some of the better rooms in the centre being occupied by servants, it is concluded to make some additions for lodging of servants and that a building be carried up betwixt the East Wing and stable to consist of two stories, one to unite with the men's Gallery on the ground floor and the other with the women's gallery above.[74]

MORAL TREATMENT AS DISCOMFORTING

Despite the fact that patients sometimes remained at The Retreat even after they were 'recovered' because of its indulgent lifestyle, there were also negative aspects of life at the institution. The records show that heroic measures were not abandoned as Samuel Tuke claimed in his *Description of The Retreat*. Perhaps the benefits of The Retreat were better than alternative situations; many patients were apparently willing to suffer some 'bleedings' or 'purges' to escape the even more terrible living conditions often found in the private madhouses or large public institutions. Even though a few families accused The Retreat of allowing less than perfect conditions to exist, most families were elated with the degree of difference in the quality of the care that their relatives received in contrast to that of previous circumstances.

Numerous medicines and utensils were purchased by The Retreat, including those for heroic treatment. In 1796 and 1797, for example, there were receipts that stated:

> Revd of Wm Tuke 7 pounds, 2 shillings, and 8 pence for Druggs for the Retreat bye Francis Theakston: Tart Emetic Zi in 6, Jallap Z Cr Tartar, Jallap Ziz Calomel . . . Blister for Ann Reston, Sinctar for Ann Retton, Camphor, Mixture Antimoneae, Mixture for Mrs. King, Cathartic Mixture . . . Calomel, Blister for M. Evans, Pills of ammoniated Copper, Chalybeate Pills . . .[75] Laud. Liq, Extract Liq. Camp., Pewter Ear Syringe, Antimonial Emetic, Mercurial Purgon, Turned Orange Pease, Astringent mixture, Blistering Plaister=Large Skin . . .[76] 14 Pint Flint Bottles, 25 Halfpint, 9 six ounce, 5 six ounce with brass covers, 7 three ounce stopper vials, mortar and Pestle . . . and 1 oz. Magnesia Calomel, 34 oz. tin powder, 4 oz. Ethiops Mineral, 34 oz. Crabs Eyes, 31 oz. precipitate sulphur antimony, 34 oz. steel wire, 36 oz. oil caroway seeds, 31 oz. tartar emetic, 73 oz. Extract Peruvian Bark . . .[77]

Similar records, relatively constant in content, are found for virtually every year of the first two decades.

Heroic drugs were not just purchased; they were definitely used. In 1807, Margaret Baynes, a servant, was fond of 'sing and dance and antic motions. . . . Has had mustard cataplasms to feet and been blistered in head, shoulders, and legs and been bled thrice by leeches and thrice by lancet . . . in good health but much reduced by means used'.[78] In 1796, Mary Evans' medicine had to be forced into her mouth and Mary Bayes was 'bled and blistered and emetics repeated . . . relief short in duration'.[79] John Young strangled himself in the night with 'an old silk handkerchief'. He had made no attempt to injure self or others and, in 1798, treatment was tried including 'change of air, company, blisters, cathartics, bleeding by leeches, bark, salt water, bathing by advice of physician but to no avail'.[80]

John Walton was 'kept at bay by strong stimulants'.[81] Ann Brown talked of killing herself and children but, in 1805, she improved with 'warm baths and opium pills in ale at bedtime'.[82] Tuke wrote in his *Description* that large meals were used to induce sleep instead of opium, but this record clearly refutes his statement. Phebe Tanner had 'erroneous notions . . . thought bewitched . . . little sleep . . . given blisters, sinopisms, internal medecines [sic] . . . not desired effect . . . discontinued medecine [sic]'.[83] The Retreat apparently realized the sometimes injurious impact of heroic treatment, but it may have been as dependent on this option as the neighboring madhouses of the time.

Other records contribute further to the picture of a less than perfect setting. It was proposed that 'some part of the shed beyond the men's dining room' be made into a convenient apartment for disorderly men patients. (A note in the margin called this a secluding room.)[84] One woman wrote to complain because 'the Gallery patients were in a stench that was abominable. Many of the poor objects are to the last degree loathsome and disgusting! My mind hurt on my father's account that he should be locked up with such company. If director knows and does not attend . . . sinful neglect'.[85] Accounts of the patients include notes that Ann Wallas was 'Pushed by M. Both in the Airing court. . . . Fell and bruised her head'.[86] John Baker was described as striking other patients and 'on such occasions it is found proper to put on the strait waistcoat for a day or two. . .'.[87] Physical restraint was employed for significant time periods. Nathaniel Samms died of suicide strangulation in 1805,[88] and there were three suicides in the first few years of The Retreat's operation alone.

However, despite the fact that it wasn't perfect, the balance of the evidence does suggest that treatment was less violent or radical than at most other institutions. Warm baths were used frequently with women patients, and this method may actually have been beneficial in terms of relaxation and hygiene. Elizabeth Ivison had 'tendency to refuse food . . . was bled in arm . . . more injurious than beneficial . . . has deranged brother . . . warm bath useful'.[89] Ann Mavity 'accused self of great crimes . . . penurious in disposition . . . twice attempted to strangle self . . . used warm bath in this state'.[90] In two cases for women patients, bleeding appeared of no use but 'the warm bath appeared to contribute to recovery'.[91] It is written that a warm bath helped Mary Webster who was frantic and biting and striking the attendants.[92] Sarah Filby suffered from 'excessive uterine haemorrhage . . . warm bath useful'.[93]

Causes of Insanity

The archives are especially illuminating in recording the extent to which diagnoses of diseases or disorders were informed by Quaker values, particularly given the uncertainties surrounding the understanding of the causes of insanity in the 18th and early 19th centuries. Causes were often thought to be of an external nature rather than of internal organic origins. Examples of external causes include that attributed to Elizabeth Waring's disease: 'Cause of present situation seems to have been a stress ocasioned [*sic*] by some thieves attempting my Neighbor's House. . . . Saw 2 men in night in neighbor's garden conversing in manner completely incomprehensible . . . lost rest . . . received medecines [*sic*] didn't help'.[94] Ann Willis was 'deserted by man when young and falling into low circumstances contributed much to her disorder'.[95] James Pritchett's 'current derangement from having been much embarrassed and perplexed by a close attention to the discharge of a trusteeship in the case of two Friends whose affairs were deranged'.[96] A young woman's 'mind was supposed to have been turned by seeing a tragedy acted out at the playhouse, where she first was thrown into strong convulsions by seeing of it, this about 4 years since'.[97] Henry Wormall was 'confined in York Castle for ecclesiastical demands for 10 years and before'.[98] Perhaps imprisonment and persecution were contributing causes of insanity among many Quakers.

Several letters stated that lunacy was caused by intemperance, a physical and at the same time moral cause.[99] Joseph Collier showed

> great propensity for learning from child . . . eminence in profession as Surgeon . . . active Member of the Meetings of Malcontents during French Revolution and tried for sedition . . . too liberal use of liquor . . . mania . . . father insane . . .[100]

Ruth Sheffield was a servant who had 'fear in the night of people entering with bad intent. . . . father had similar problem . . . voracious appetite . . . fond of strong drink'.[101] Sibylla Turnour was 'hypochondriacal . . . excited by stimulants (wine). . . . strong propensity toward stimulants . . . irritable'.[102] Numerous other examples in addition to these histories seem readily to refute Samuel Tuke's claim that only three cases at The Retreat were due to intemperance.

Friends were particularly concerned with the notion of the hereditary cause of insanity because of the Quaker requirement to 'marry in the Society'. Admitees were often described as having insanity of 'a family nature'. Patient cases were each assigned a number and these numbers were used when listing relatives who were currently or had at one time been patients at The Retreat. John Fawcett's was a 'Family complaint' and his brother was Josh Fawcett #387.[103] Hannah Woodville was the sister of Susannah #216.[104] Mary Prideaux was the aunt to William Prideaux #112, and Samuel Clemensha was the father of P. T. Bleckly #371 and Robert Clemensha. Ann Wallis was the sister of Elizabeth W. #77.[105] Her grandmother was 'many years of a melancholy and gloomy habit. Her mother who died was of a gloomy turn of mind. . . . 4 sisters . . . 3 of them are not quite like other people. . .'.[106] Elizabeth Waring was the sister of Samuel #5 and Mary #10.[107]

As mentioned in an earlier context, women patients were often thought to have disorders related to the uterus, a medical model of insanity. It was recorded in 1802 that Sarah Filby 'aged 45 years came under my care in month of May last on account of debility and hurry of spirits, there is great reason to believe in consequence of uterine haemorrhage; and by use of nervine and tonic medecines [sic] her constitution became so much ammended [sic], that hopes were entertained of relief from the various false ideas and impressions to which she was subject but unfortunately of late, those symptoms wear [sic] the most serious and threatening aspect and render her proper object. . . .'.[108]

Significantly, a number of patients' disorders were thought to be due to iatrogenic causes, especially the 'improper use of mercury'[109] in medical treatment. John Alexander feared poison and abstained from food for several days and his disorder was thought to have been brought about by 'improper use of mercury'.[110] Robert Lampert was thought to be insane as a result of 'too profuse application of mercury for tumour on his nose. . . . during paroxysm there is frequently copious discharge of thin mucous from nose . . . incoherent, impatient, flighty, grave, factious, costive, tongue white . . . powerful emetic used'.[111]

Other disorders were linked to fever. A relative of one patient wrote: 'think what first induced it was hearing the noises of an insane person 6 years ago. . . . a brain fever soon followed which lasted 6 weeks. . . . I cannot find that any of her family were afflicted with this malady'.[112] William Gillespie's disorder was also attributed by his doctor to 'being in too hot a climate (he had traveled to South Carolina) and disappointment in business having had the Yellow Fever at the same time'.[113] T. Remmington was 'supposed to be materially affected by a violent fever'.[114]

Diagnoses reflected concerns within the Society. Quakers tended to attribute many disorders to external physical causes such as falling down, having a fever, overdrinking, or being treated with the improper use of mercury. Of these causes, 'alcoholic overindulgence' clearly foreshadowed the eventual rejection of alcohol, even in moderate quantities, by the Quaker Society of the time. By labeling those who drank too much as 'insane', the Society of Friends could invalidate these individuals just as society had attempted to invalidate the Society of Friends by calling Quakers 'mad'.

Worry about the hereditary basis of madness also reflects concerns that were present in the Quaker community about the consequences of 'marrying in'. Further, the frequent adherence to 'uterine' theories of insanity in female patients suggests that, although the Society preached the equality of women, it also shared, on some level, the larger societal belief in the biological instability (read: inferiority) of the female sex. Finally, the fact that disorders with external causes were believed to be treatable by 'moral' measures suggests an acceptance of a mind/body unity that was in contrast to the standard dualistic model of madness held by most medical doctors at the time (cf. William Bynum's article 'Rationales for British Therapy in British Psychiatry, 1780-1835' in *Madhouses, Mad-doctors, Madmen*).

Symptoms of Insanity

In addition to causes, examining records of symptoms of insanity is also useful in casting light on the way 18th and 19th century Quakers viewed mental illness. Violence was a common symptom. Thomas Mair's paroxysms 'come on generally at his first going to bed . . . became much agitated in his sleep . . . attempted opening the window shutters . . . tears clothes'.[115] One man made an attempt on his own life and that of a young woman, and Francis Fox 'made some attempt to injure his wife or to raise her fear'.[116] Patients often had suicidal symptoms. One widower frequently 'reflected against herself'.[117] Mary Dearmen made 'an attempt on her life with a razor, which she had somehow secreted'.[118] Another woman 'made an attempt by taking laudanum to deprive herself of existence . . . effect prevented by speedy dose of emetic'.[119]

Other cases showed typical symptoms of depression. Regarding a patient Prideaux, it was written that 'the disorder shows itself chiefly by a great degree of indolence and a desire to lay mostly in bed'.[120] Another was described as having a disorder 'rather of the melancholy kind'.[121] There was also the symptom of refusing food. Hannah Bradshaw was 'exceedingly agitated at times, at others very dejected and distressed . . . increased derangement . . . no sleep . . . no food for nearly 10 days . . . total abstinence from solids, liquids, and sleep. . . . 2 strong people . . . to manage her onto chaise in London with a straitwaist coat on and feet confined'.[122] Additionally, there were examples of paranoid symptoms such as the man who was 'harrassed [*sic*] with the idea of a bandit being lying in wait for him about to attack him . . . pushed bedstead against door to prevent as he said some persons from coming to murder him. He added he thought he had no alternative but that of submitting or jumping out of the window'.[123] Some patients apparently also heard voices. Robert Pope wrote about a Member of his Meeting who 'fancies hearing strange voices within which prompt him to action'.[124]

Other symptoms were considerably different from those which we are accustomed to facing today. Costiveness, the term used for constipation, was assumed to be a symptom of insanity. One Jane Bigland, insane, 'had very obstinate costiveness and she was ordered to be frequently carried into the open air [from] which she at first seemed to derive some advantage . . .'.[125] B. Wilmer, MD, wrote of Mary Nickson, 'Symptoms attending her unhappy situation have been chiefly of the nervous kind: viz. pain of the head, watchfulness, pains and spasms of the stomach, and of the muscles in general; indigestion, flatulence, costiveness, and a deranged state of the stomach and bowels. . .'.[126]

Excessive writing was also thought to be a symptom of insanity, especially pernicious because it encouraged brooding upon one's insane thoughts. A father wrote, 'I was sorry to find he continued in practice of writing so much as it may sometimes prevent him from walking and other exercise useful for him'.[127] Daniel Olives wrote of another patient, 'it would be better if she had no opportunity of writing. . . . I had a letter from her 10 days ago full of incoherent stuff'.[128] In a related case, Thomas Broadbent Bland was thought to be insane and one of his symptoms was 'taking poetry too literally'.[129]

Religious symptoms were exceedingly common, particularly among women patients. One woman was said to be accustomed to speak 'improperly in Meeting and hav[e] strange visionary whims'.[130] Ann Sawton 'at Meeting laid claim to revelation as to clearly express her disorder'.[131] Another woman is described: 'Spoke in Meeting . . . not an acknowledged minister . . . thoughts of a weak capacity'.[132] Of Mary Pyle it was written, 'Spoke in Meetings. . . . Not an acknowledged minister as some thought . . . absurd ideas. . . . no expectation of marriage'.[133] Mary Bayes was claimed to be '. . . in [the] habit of speaking in Meeting . . . not a minister.'[134] Sarah Delves was an 'acknowledged minister', but she married out of the Society.[135] Patience King was known to have 'imaginary religious scruples . . . wears cap and keeps sabbath on 5th day lying in bed'.[136] Sarah Filby's disorder was characterized by the fact that she 'Spoke in Meetings' and Elizabeth Wallis had 'religious peculiarities . . . consulted Bible on ordinary things. . .'.[137] Mary Benwell 'had strained nerves from religious subjects'.[138] Martha Dickinson was thought to have 'erroneous religious ideas . . . dangerous impact on conduct . . . spoke in Meetings in eccentric way'.[139] Elizabeth Sims was recorded as a 'Convinced Friend with an obstinate refusal to take food from an apprehended religious principle. . .'.[140]

These cases clearly refute Samuel Tuke's *Description* in which he states that patients at The Retreat, in contrast to those of other institutions, did not suffer from religiously-inspired forms of insanity. Moreover, the cases are significant in their revelation about attitudes toward women in the community. Perhaps the Quakers preached equality, but apparently when women 'spoke up too much' at least some were vulnerable to being labeled as insane.

There were two specific references to 'moral' symptoms of insanity. Samuel Myers 'Rests little at night. . . . Bad women and evil spirits bother. . . . Readmitted with moral insanity emerging in a sullen and suspicious monomania'.[141] Mary Nickson had

> great sleeplessness which resisted anodynes . . . drops of rosemary given by Jepson . . . case of moral insanity . . . stingy and ill-natured . . . starved children and henpecked husband . . . feigned fits of epilepsy . . . buried at The Retreat worn out by disease.[142]

The asylum staff compared symptoms of insanity seeking to find patterns of syndromes that could be categorized and studied. Rachel Hallpike's case was compared to Margaret Willis' case.[143] Sarah Harris' case was described as 'the counterpart of Samuel Waring #85. . . . Father deranged or eccentric'.[144] John Coning was 'melancholy' and medicine was 'no help and not usually for this kind of patient . . . readmitted into Appendage . . . case resembles Samuel Myers . . . wife is wicked and abominable. . .'.[145]

Conclusion

Careful examination of the archives from the first two decades of The Retreat's founding and operation demonstrates above all else that there is no definitive answer to the historiographical question of what 'moral treatment' really was – a moral liberation or moral imprisonment. As Anne Digby states, The Retreat was in reality 'Janus-faced'. Beginning with the Quaker versus non-Quaker admission debate, the records leave us questioning. Although The Retreat did accept non-Quakers, those patients who were non-Friends paid higher rates. In addition, it turns out that many of the 'non-Quakers' had in fact been Members at one time. It appears that there may have been an easy progression from dismissing Members who deviated from the rules to labeling them 'mad'.

Staff were supposedly integrated into 'The Family', and yet a reasonably high turnover rate for employees indicates that for them, at least, The Retreat was not a 'quiet haven' suggesting home. Women staff were at times treated as equals in terms of salary, but on other points they seem to have been marginal or insignificant – as in the decision-making processes of The Retreat. For female patients, speaking out in Meeting was not infrequently considered symptomatic of mental instability, but there was no parallel diagnosis evident for males.

There is also the question of how much moral treatment actually reflected an ideological reaction against a somatic medical orientation in the 'management' of the mad. Staff routinely requested medical certificates and employed virtually all the heroic treatments represented in the medical repertoire of the day. Yet, in their practice, they certainly gave major attention both to psychological and religious postures as well.

In respect to the physical setting, The Retreat strove earnestly to 'humanize' the living conditions available to the mad. At the same time, however, many of the improvements were steeped in class consciousness. How do we reconcile the avowed intent to enhance patient accommodations with the records of the terrible smells present in the asylum galleries and the all too numerous suicides? Did The Retreat overindulge wealthy patients with fine food, accommodations, and alcohol in order to keep them happy in an extravagant setting that little prepared them for the outside world, or did it seek to reintegrate patients into the larger society through 'tea parties', exercise, gardening, and occupational therapy?

We are left then juxtaposing the stench of the living quarters, leeches, and antimonial emetics with the elegance of mahogany dressers, ivory combs, and French brandy. Perhaps some insight into the contradictions inherent in moral treatment will come from an examination of the philosophy which created and underlay it. The evolution of Quakerism provides a previously unused lens with which to view moral therapy in the context of The York Retreat.

Notes

[1] Borthwick Institute of Historical Research, *The Archives of The York Retreat. A Summary List* (Borthwick Institute, 1975), p. 1. (Xeroxed handout – available at BIHR).
[2] BIHR, Case Book, 1st of 2nd month, 1798.
[3] BIHR, Directors' Rough Minute Book, 1792-1841, p. 1.
[4] BIHR, Directors' Rough Minute Book, pp. 1-7.
[5] BIHR, Directors' Minute Book, 1792-1841, p. 7.
[6] BIHR, Directors' Rough Minute Book, pp. 1-2.
[7] BIHR, Special Brochure, p. 7.
[8] BIHR, Directors' Minute Book, p. 11.
[9] BIHR, Directors' Minute Book, p. 26.
[10] BIHR, Case Book, 13th of 6th month, 1796.
[11] BIHR, Directors' Minute Book, p. 27.
[12] BIHR, Directors' Minute Book, p. 32.
[13] BIHR, Committee Report, 29th of 10th month, 1798, pp. 26-27.
[14] BIHR, Committee Report, 3rd of 5th month, 1799, pp. 29-30.
[15] BIHR, Committee Report, 28th of 4th month, 1800, p. 35.
[16] BIHR, Committee Report, 23rd of 6th month, 1800, p. 36.
[17] BIHR, Committee Report, 2nd of 5th month, 1802, p. 49.
[18] BIHR, Committee Report, 30th of 5th month, 1805, p. 78.
[19] BIHR, H. C. Hunt, Summary of The Retreat History, Summary of Correspondence, Vol. 1.
[20] BIHR, Directors' Minute Book, p. 12.
[21] BIHR, Committee Report, 28th of 8th month, 1809, p. 102.

[22] BIHR, Correspondence, 31st of 4th month, 1799.
[23] BIHR, Correspondence, 24th of 9th month, 1802.
[24] BIHR, Directors' Minute Book, p.46.
[25] BIHR, Directors' Minute Book, p.51.
[26] BIHR, Committee Report, 26th of 9th month, 1808, p.95.
[27] BIHR, Correspondence, 11th of 10th month, 1805.
[28] BIHR, Correspondence, 21st of 1st month, 1810.
[29] BIHR, Correspondence, 17th of 8th month, 1796.
[30] BIHR, Correspondence, 30th of 11th month, 1796.
[31] BIHR, Committee Report, 23rd of 5th month, 1796, pp.2-4.
[32] BIHR, Directors' Minute Book, p.18.
[33] BIHR, Committee Report, 14th of 4th month and 26th of 6th month, 1796, pp.14-17.
[34] BIHR, Committee Report, 27th of 7th month, 1801, p.44.
[35] BIHR, Committee Report, 30th of 8th month, 1802, p.51.
[36] BIHR, Committee Report, 31st of 7th month, 1797, pp.15-17.
[37] BIHR, Directors' Minute Book, p.70.
[38] BIHR, Directors' Minute Book, p.83.
[39] BIHR, Committee Report, 9th of 5th month, 1796, pp.2-4.
[40] BIHR, Committee Report, 25th of 7th month, 1796, pp.6-7.
[41] BIHR, Committee Report, 31st of 8th month, 1812, p.127.
[42] BIHR, Committee Report, 29th of 7th month, 1811, p.117.
[43] BIHR, Retreat Brochure, 17th of 1st month, 1796, p.22.
[44] BIHR, Committee Report, 25th of 7th month, 1796, pp.7-8.
[45] BIHR, Retreat Brochure, 17th of 1st month, 1796, p.22.
[46] BIHR, Directors' Minute Book, p.37.
[47] BIHR, Directors' Minute Book, p.41.
[48] BIHR, Committee Report, 6th of 6th month, 1803, p.57.
[49] BIHR, Correspondence, 27th of 6th month, 1800.
[50] BIHR, Directors' Minute Book, p.32.
[51] BIHR, Correspondence, 10th of 4th month, 1799.
[52] For an analysis of women and mental health in 18th-century England see Elizabeth Showalter's *The Female Malady* (New York: Pantheon Books, 1985).
[53] BIHR, Committee Report, 1799.
[54] BIHR, Correspondence, 17th of 8th month, 1796.
[55] BIHR, Correspondence, 25th of 7th month, 1802.
[56] BIHR, Correspondence, 24th of 9th month, 1802.
[57] BIHR, Directors' Minute Book, p.28.
[58] BIHR, Committee Report, 24th of 9th month, 1804, p.68.
[59] BIHR, Committee Report, 2nd of 3rd month, 1811, p.114.
[60] BIHR, Correspondence, 14th of 11th month, 1802.
[61] BIHR, Correspondence, 22nd of 2nd month, 1779.
[62] BIHR, Committee Report, 27th of 6th month, 1803, p.57.
[63] BIHR, Committee Report, 29th of 2nd month, 1808, p.89.
[64] BIHR, Committee Report, 7th of 6th month, 1808, p.92.
[65] BIHR, Committee Report, 14th of 4th month, 1797, pp.14-15.
[66] BIHR, Committee Report, 31st of 1st month, 1804, p.62.
[67] BIHR, Special Brochure, Directors' Minute Book, 1794, p.7.
[68] BIHR, Building of The Retreat, 1794.
[69] BIHR, Building of The Retreat, 11th of 3rd month, 1797.
[70] BIHR, Building of The Retreat, 21st of 3rd month, 1796.

[71] BIHR, Building of The Retreat, 7th of 9th month, 1796.
[72] BIHR, Building of The Retreat, Oct.-Jan., 1808.
[73] BIHR, Directors' Minute Book, p.32.
[74] BIHR, Committee Report, 10th of 9th month, 1812, p.128.
[75] BIHR, Building of The Retreat, Receipt dated 21st of 12th month, 1796.
[76] BIHR, Building of The Retreat, Receipts from Sept.-Feb., 1796.
[77] BIHR, Building of The Retreat, Receipt dated 25th of 8th month, 1797.
[78] BIHR, Case Book, 29th of 1st month, 1807.
[79] BIHR, Case Book, 4th of 8th month, 1796.
[80] BIHR, Case Book, 27th of 11th month, 1798.
[81] BIHR, Case Book, 23rd of 9th month, 1796.
[82] BIHR, Case Book, 4th of 5th month, 1805.
[83] BIHR, Case Book, 12th of 10th month, 1807.
[84] BIHR, Committee Report, 26th of 3rd month and 30th of 4th month, 1804, pp.63-64.
[85] BIHR, Correspondence, 27th of 10th month, 1812.
[86] BIHR, Case Book, 28th of 10th month, 1798.
[87] BIHR, Case Book, 24th of 11th month, 1798.
[88] BIHR, Case Book, 13th of 12th month, 1798.
[89] BIHR, Case Book, 29th of 10th month, 1808.
[90] BIHR, Case Book, 18th of 6th month, 1808.
[91] BIHR, Case Book, 20th of 10th month and 21st of 11th month, 1801.
[92] BIHR, Case Book, 2nd of 3rd month, 1802.
[93] BIHR, Case Book, 25th of 9th month, 1802.
[94] BIHR, Correspondence, 1801.
[95] BIHR, Correspondence, 21st of 8th month, 1802.
[96] BIHR, Correspondence, 19th of 5th month, 1803.
[97] BIHR, Correspondence, 1803.
[98] BIHR, Case Book, 11th of 9th month, 1808.
[99] BIHR, Correspondence, 6th of 8th month, 1797.
[100] BIHR, Case Book, 4th of 6th month, 1806.
[101] BIHR, Case Book, 2nd of 1st month, 1808.
[102] BIHR, Case Book, 8th of 9th month, 1812.
[103] BIHR, Case Book, 1st of 2nd month, 1798.
[104] BIHR, Case Book, 13th of 9th month, 1799.
[105] BIHR, Case Book, 25th of 3rd month, 5th of 9th month, and 28th of 10th month, 1798.
[106] BIHR, Correspondence, 19th of 7th month, 1805.
[107] BIHR, Case Book, 27th of 11th month, 1801.
[108] BIHR, Certificates, 22nd of 6th month, 1802, p.45.
[109] BIHR, Correspondence, 27th of 8th month, 1804.
[110] BIHR, Case Book, 13th of 6th month, 1804.
[111] BIHR, Case Book, 1805.
[112] BIHR, Correspondence, 3rd of 8th month, 1804.
[113] BIHR, Correspondence, 26th of 5th month, 1804.
[114] BIHR, Correspondence, 17th of 1st month, 1806.
[115] BIHR, Correspondence, 11th of 3rd month, 1797.
[116] BIHR, Correspondence, 13th of 8th month, 1809, and 22nd of 10th month, 1810.
[117] BIHR, Correspondence, 6th of 12th month, 1797.
[118] BIHR, Correspondence, 2nd of 3rd month and 10th of 4th month, 1800.

119 BIHR, Correspondence, 13th of 7th month, 1808.
120 BIHR, Correspondence, 2nd of 8th month, 1798.
121 BIHR, Correspondence, 6th of 12th month, 1798.
122 BIHR, Correspondence, 21st of 7th month, 1799.
123 BIHR, Correspondence, 11th of 2nd month, 1811.
124 BIHR, Correspondence, 8th of 5th month, 1800.
125 BIHR, Certificates, 17th of 10th month, 1801, p. 36.
126 BIHR, Certificates, 1812.
127 BIHR, Correspondence, 18th of 8th month, 1798.
128 BIHR, Correspondence, 21st of 8th month, 1811.
129 BIHR, Case Book, 28th of 10th month, 1800.
130 BIHR, Correspondence, 3rd of 10th month and 10th of 12th month, 1807.
131 BIHR, Correspondence, 22nd of 8th month, 1808.
132 BIHR, Case Book, 22nd of 7th month, 1796.
133 BIHR, Case Book, 12th of 8th month, 1796.
134 BIHR, Case Book, 1796.
135 BIHR, Case Book, 6th of 12th month, 1796.
136 BIHR, Case Book, 20th of 3rd month, 25th of 9th month, and 7th of 11th month, 1802.
137 BIHR, Case Book, 20th of 3rd month, 25th of 9th month, and 7th of 11th month, 1802.
138 BIHR, Case Book, 31st of 7th month, 1802.
139 BIHR, Case Book, 10th of 7th month, 1804.
140 BIHR, Case Book, 25th of 1st month, 1805.
141 BIHR, Case Book, 10th of 7th month, 1802.
142 BIHR, Case Book, 1812.
143 BIHR, Case Book, 16th of 12th month, 1800.
144 BIHR, Case Book, 2nd of 4th month, 1805.
145 BIHR, Case Book, 10th of 7th month, 1804.

Huc Fecit

Amicorum Charitas, in humanitatis

Arvgumentum.

Anno Dñr MDCCXCII

'For the love of Friends this was done as evidence of humanity. 1792.'
*William Tuke's own handwriting at the foot of the original document
expressing the sentiments which inspired the work of the founders of
The Retreat.*

*George Fox 1624-1691,
founder of the Quaker
Movement in 1652*

AFTER A PAINTING
BY SAMUEL CHINN

*William Tuke 1732-1822,
founder of
The York Retreat, 1792.
Opened in 1796*

FROM THE PAINTING
BY HENRY SCOTT TUKE, RA

CHAPTER THREE

The Quaker Context:
The Role of Quakerism in The Retreat
Asylum Reform

'And Friends to have and provide a house for them that be *distempered and not to go out into the world*. And to have an almshouse or hospital for all poor Friends, that are past work. . . . The poor, the sick, the widows, the fatherless, the prisoners be tender of, and feel everyone's condition as your own, and let nothing be lacking amongst you, according to the apostle's doctrine of the Church of God of old time; and if nothing is lacking all is well . . . know in all your meetings who is sick, and weak, and in want, and widowless, and fatherless, and aged people who cannot help themselves . . . lay aside for the necessity of others, as you are moved and commanded of the Lord God by his power and spirit; for he that gives to the poor, lendeth to the Lord; and he loves a cheerful giver'.[1] – George Fox, Epistles, 1669.

'Whatever temptations, distractions, confusions the light does make manifest and discover, do not look at these temptations, confusions, corruptions; but look at the Light which discovers them. . . . For looking down at sin and corruption ye are swallowed up in it but looking at the Light which discovers them, ye will see over them'. – George Fox to Oliver Cromwell's daughter, Lady Claypole, who was 'sick and much troubled in mind'.[3]

George Fox, founder of the Quaker movement in the northwest of England in 1652,[3] wrote of the need for a place for the 'distempered' more than a century before William Tuke founded The Retreat in York, England in 1796. In his letter to Lady Claypole, Fox suggested the curability of insanity by stating that if she followed the 'Light', she would see over the sin and corruption which caused her to be 'troubled in mind'.

In explaining the origin of The York Retreat, historians have neglected this century gap between the ideas of George Fox and the founding of The

49

Retreat in 1796. Why did Quakers wait until the 18th century to carry out the 17th-century idea of a 'house' where the insane might be cured? What motivated and allowed William Tuke to carry Fox's original ideas into practice? Historians have focused mainly on the immediate impetus for The Retreat's beginnings – the death of a Quaker woman, Hannah Mills, under suspicious circumstances at the York Asylum on the '30th of the 4th month, 1790'.[4] Beyond this event, historians such as Mary Glover, William and Margaret Sessions, Andrew Scull, and Anne Digby[5] often cite only one Quaker tenet – the belief in the existence of 'that God in every person' – as an additional motivation for the humane care of the insane. These explanations, however, fail to make clear why Quakers of an earlier period, who shared the same core beliefs as Tuke, did not carry their religious ideals into action for reform in the care of the mentally ill. Seventeenth-century Quakers undoubtedly encountered firsthand the mistreatment of the insane when they suffered prison sentences during the years of their religious persecution,[6] but they did not act for reform on their behalf.

It is my conviction that examining Quakerism as a process instead of simply as a set of fixed beliefs will allow a more satisfactory explanation of William Tuke's initial founding of The Retreat and the rise of moral treatment therein. Focusing on those aspects of Quakerism most relevant to the understanding of the story of The Retreat, this chapter will examine 150 years of the Friends movement, dividing its evolution into two separate periods: 1650-1700 (the heroic period), and 1700-1800 (period of conservatism, organization, and Quietism).[7]

This chapter will be divided into two sections. Part one traces the beginnings of Quakerism from 1650-1700, and outlines parallels between Quaker beliefs and The Retreat's founding and functioning. The second section begins with an explanation of the development of Quaker ideology from 1700-1800, and describes the changing structure of the Society's governance. Finally, the development of Quakerism in the 18th century is placed in parallel with The Retreat's practices.

Part One
The Beginnings of Quakerism: The Heroic Period

1650-1700: A Reactionary Phenomenon with Emphasis on Inner Discipline

The period 1650 to 1700 can be characterized by the development of Quakerism as a reactionary phenomenon. George Fox and other Quakers sought to form a religion based on the primary experience of that measure of

God within each person. The Society of Friends wanted a religious sect based on inward reflection rather than outward ceremony.[8] For Quakers, Catholics relied too centrally on ecclesiastical hierarchy, and Protestants, while rejecting the authority of the church, relied too heavily on the Bible as the best way to know God. George Fox and his followers believed it was more important to experience directly what God was saying than to read about what He once said centuries ago.[9] The Quaker religious movement stressed the need to do away with ritual in order to experience firsthand what Fox referred to as the 'Light Within' or the 'Light of Christ', given to each individual regardless of sex, class, race, or mental state.[10] The process of experiencing the Light Within took place in a silent Meeting for Worship in which the individual moved gradually from 'convincement' of the existence of the Light to 'conversion', a long struggle through which inward discipline gradually humbled the human will to the will of God.[11]

Moral Treatment of 1790: A Reactionary Phenomenon with Emphasis on Inner Discipline

The Quakerism of the 1650's, often viewed as a negative phenomenon and as a 'stripping-down' of old tradition along with a strong belief in inward discipline, found renewed expression in the development of moral treatment a century and a half later at The York Retreat. Anne Harrington, Assistant Professor of the History of Science at Harvard University, stated in a 1990 lecture that moral treatment must be 'first and foremost . . . understood as a negative phenomenon, an attempt to provide an alternative to the chains and other restraints of the traditional madhouses. The watchword of the new approach was restraint without chains – chains would be eliminated because the patient would be taught to restrain himself'.[12] The parallels with the ideals of Quaker reformism are striking. From the very beginning of the Quaker movement, Friends challenged ecclesiastical hierarchy and rejected the outward ceremonies of the traditional Christian church. They were willing to be nonconformist in the social sphere and even suffered imprisonment for their convictions. In instituting moral treatment for The Retreat patients, William Tuke and his followers similarly dared to strip away the traditional brutal treatment of the insane as animals. This was not as complete a 'stripping away' of all heroic treatment as Tuke, Zilboorg, Glover, and the Sessions have argued. Some heroic treatments were still practiced and physical restraints were employed as mentioned in Chapter Two, but on the whole The Retreat's 'moral treatment' represented a radical reduction in harshness as a method for treating the insane. On this point, the Sessions were correct when they wrote that in an 'era which did not consider positive treatment for the mentally afflicted possible . . . William's project was entirely beyond the bounds of most people's conception. . . '.[13] Early Quakerism and its followers set the stage for a later play. William Tuke would successfully use the Quaker tradition of following the Inner Light in spite of the unpopularity and suffering that the leading might bring. In a sense, the ideological foundation for moral treatment was present from the start of the movement; the actual reform, however, would have to wait until the 1790's, when change became possible through economic growth and the rise of new leadership.

The Founder: George Fox and the Inner Light Experienced

Fox, the organizational genius of the Quaker movement and revered public Friend, spread his truth by preaching. His goal, though, was to 'bring people . . . to the end of all preaching'.[14] According to Philadelphia Yearly Meeting, Fox was a 'powerful, prophetic personality and a born leader. . . . nothing could quench [his] ardor or chain [his] spiritual power'.[15] He often believed that he spoke directly to God, receiving answers and guidance.[16] He led mass meetings with 'fiery emotions'.[17] At the center of Fox's message was the doctrine of the 'Inner Light', the Light of Christ present in each man which unites people not by external authority but by an internal spirit.[18] Unlike the Catholic Church, which felt that divinity could only be experienced at particular times such as when 'the miracle of transubstantiation is completed and the bread and wine transformed into the body and blood of Christ',[19] or the Protestant Church, which worshipped a God who had removed himself from this world, Quakers sensed a God present in the here and now through the Inner Light they believed extant in every human being. This produced a kind of Quaker mysticism, directed not only toward God but also toward mankind. The shared Light produced both a vertical relationship with God and a horizontal unity with other men. The 'vertical relation to God and the horizontal relation to man are like two co-ordinates used to plot a curve; without both the position of the curve could not be determined'.[20] This caused Quakers to be concerned about the well-being of men in this life, and helped to stimulate their efforts in asylum reform.

The Founder: William Tuke and the Inner Light Experienced

It is easy to see how a religion inspired not by God's law without but by the Light within could produce action toward social reform. William Tuke spoke of a divine inspiration emanating from his inner soul, an inspiration that pushed him toward founding The Retreat. The Sessions state that despite being nearly 60 years old,[21] Tuke felt compelled to follow his Inner Light. 'Once William Tuke had become convinced of the urgent need to improve methods of healing mental illness nothing could shake his resolve to show the way by practical example.'[22] Tuke had reached an age and economic stability at which many would have retired. Yet, the tradition of an individual experience of the divine on this earth, started years earlier by George Fox, had smitten him. He felt inwardly drawn to the cause of reform for the insane, and nothing could or would deter his 'faith and practice'.

52

The Founders: George Fox and William Tuke and the Inner Light Intellectualized

George Fox's description of the Inner Light gives an even clearer picture of how this tradition influenced William Tuke. The Light, for Fox, was superhuman and consisted of 'substance, reality, unity, and peace' as opposed to a darker earthly world of 'shadow, deceit, multiplicity, and strife'. The superhuman Light from above was eternal whereas other worldly qualities were merely temporal.[23] This Light was 'God in his capacity as creator and redeemer' and 'to live in the Light is to become God's agent in the process of creation and redemption'.[24] To live only in the Light, however, would be to deny the world, and for Quakers this was wrong. Quakerism sought both 'world-denial' and 'world-affirmation'. Ideally, a withdrawal toward the contemplation of the Light was balanced by a subsequent return to the active life; in this way, it was believed that the principle of the world might be reconciled with the Light of God.[25] It would not be sufficient, then, for William Tuke inwardly to recognize the cruelty of the treatment of the insane. He had to act by creating The Retreat.

Fox said in a letter written from prison, '. . . walk cheerfully over the world answering that of God in everyone'.[26] This became the basis for the whole Quaker theory of social comportment, and underlay the rejection of many of the violent methods of control used in treatment for the insane in other institutions. Fox believed that one could not answer 'that of God' by violent means because violence moved only the external physical world, not the internal spirit. In addition, violent methods employed in the treatment of the insane would have reduced both the patient and the user to the darker physical world mentioned earlier; force could only operate to create a superficial external unity instead of real internal unity based upon a shared Light. The idea of the Light was a source of power for William Tuke, and he wanted to use it to create a unity from within among staff, patients, and all of those affiliated with The Retreat. In addition, this 'hidden unity' was inspired by the ideal of Christ in His sinless state of resistance to temptation – again, the idea of inner discipline as opposed to external restraint or laws. These ideals of Quakerism were the theoretical basis of moral treatment. In practice, however, some external restraints were employed, perhaps because the restriction of a particularly troublesome patient helped keep things running smoothly for many others.

George Fox: Righteousness and Perfectibility

Two further doctrines of early Quakerism had an important impact on the Quaker approach to social behavior. Fox taught that righteousness was not to be imputed to men unless they were actually righteous. This set Quakerism apart from other churches that believed 'that God, because of the sacrifice of Christ, could impute Christ's righteousness to man even though he continued to sin'.[27] On the other hand, Fox believed that perfectionism and freedom from sin were possible in this world.[28] In Catholicism, man could make up for his lack of goodness by sharing in the accumulated goodness of the Church. Monks', nuns', and priests' merits could act as redemption for the group.[29] For Protestants, all men continued to sin in this world and salvation could only be found in a God external to themselves and in an afterlife. For Quakers, man united with Christ (not the church) in this world and, hence, shared vicariously in God's goodness. To follow self will was a sin, but to follow the 'leadings [of the Light] moment by moment made perfection possible'.[30]

William Tuke: Righteousness and Perfectibility Through Practice

The Quaker belief in the possibility of earthly perfectionism ('living up to the measure of Light'[31]) undoubtedly prompted William Tuke to strive for change. Indeed, he used the test of 'inner peace' to judge whether or not he should push forward with the founding of The Retreat. For Quakers, inner peace came to the individual who lived up to the divine requirement – with no fear of failure and no sense of compromise.[32] As Howard Brinton states, 'The wheel of social achievement can only turn if the axle in the middle is at rest'.[33] Historically, Friends have not hesitated to support new and unpopular undertakings as a result of their beliefs in the possibility of perfectibility and absolute righteousness in the world. They have been pioneers in the abolition of slavery, and in women's rights, prison reform, Indian relief, the peace movement, and, last but not least, mental asylum reform.[34]

George Fox and William Tuke: Shared Beliefs, Different Social Climates

The beliefs of George Fox and other Members during the 17th century were not defended at an easy price. The Quaker Act of 1662 and the Conventicle Acts of 1664 and 1670 were aimed at Friends and sought to prevent them from meeting for worship. The acts provided for the fining and/or imprisonment of Quakers.[35] The liberal religious views of the Society of Friends threatened the authority of the Church of England, and many feared that the individual mysticism of the Quakers, as well as their refusal to pay taxes to the Church, would lead to anarchy. In the 1660's, after the Conventicle Acts, 'nearly all leading Friends were in prison'.[36] This fact is interesting in relation to The Retreat in three ways.

First, since many prominent Friends were in prison at the beginning of the Quaker movement, the critical leadership necessary to start such a radical institution as The York Retreat was lacking. Friends were concerned with their own persecution, and they had little immediate energy for taking up other reformist causes.

Second, the imprisonment of Friends created an awareness of the cruelty of treatment for the insane because at the time the mentally ill were not separated from the criminally convicted but housed in prisons with them. Thousands of Quakers

> who were imprisoned and treated like common criminals during the 40 years of persecution learned by experience of the horrible condition of 17th-century prisons, dungeons and underground rooms, unventilated, overcrowded, covered with filth and alive with vermin. . . . no separation of healthy and diseased, of hardened criminals and the young or even innocent, the sane and the insane.[37]

Friends, like William Tuke's great grandfather who was 'twice imprisoned in the 1660's in the York Kidcote',[38] encountered firsthand the cruelty endemic toward the treatment of the insane, and their memories were deep and long.

Third, the imprisonment of Quakers was often accompanied by the imposition of heavy fines or loss of property. Thus, the formation of a 'house' for the insane would not have been economically feasible early in the Friends movement. Indeed, 'for a century after the Act of Toleration [1689] Friends continued to suffer heavy losses through fines and imprisonment. . . '.[39] The persecution of the Society can be said to have lasted until about 1789, just one year before the death of Hannah Mills and three years before William Tuke began to propose his Retreat. It was probably one of the first times in the movement's history that the resources and leadership among Quakers were sufficient to see such a plan through to completion.

George Fox and William Tuke: Economic and Employment Disadvantages Made Positive

In addition to the Quaker Act and Conventicle Acts, the Test Act of 1673[40] 'barred . . . nonconformists from all public office, politics and university education, so that the field of professional and political occupations was severely narrowed for Friends. They refused by their own accord to enter the army or navy, leaving still fewer career paths open'.[41] Many became businessmen, but they would not deal in 'superfluities' because of the Quaker belief in seeking simplicity.[42] The Tukes were first blacksmiths and then grocers, and William Tuke continued in this latter tradition by becoming a tea merchant. Despite the restrictions, Quakers became successful in their businesses because the public trusted them to sell their products at fair prices. Arthur Raistrick writes, 'One effect of the constant persecution and derision to which the Quakers were subjected, was to make them strive to demonstrate their real integrity and trust-worthiness. They endeavored to prove by their actions in trade that they were anxious to serve the legitimate needs of their fellow men, to provide them with good quality goods at a fair price, [and] to invent and produce better and more useful articles'.[43] He adds, it was the 'unshakeable honesty of the Quaker that made people willing to place their money in his hands when most other people were suspect, and which opened the way for the success of the Quaker bankers' (for example, the Barclays and Lloyds Banks of London).[44] The eminent Cadbury and Rowntree confectioners were Quaker merchants and the latter, when joined with the Tukes (grocers) and their Retreat, gave York its reputation as the city of 'lunatics and lollipops'.[45]

The Quaker experience of professional limitation had profound implications for the founding of The Retreat. Because Quakers were pushed out of the political and educational spheres from the very beginning, there remained only social work as an outlet for their reforming zeal. Life as a tea merchant afforded William Tuke a certain amount of economic stability as well as considerable flexibility in his day-to-day schedule. In '1779 the tea business was prospering, William having the firm and able assistance of his son Henry'.[46] All of this combined contributed to the feasibility of Tuke's undertaking. In fact, he served as superintendent himself for one full year without pay.[47] Ironically, the business William inherited, originally chosen because it was about the only option available, created the economic position necessary to make a radical reform like The Retreat a reality.

Henry Tuke, 1755-1814, eldest son of William and Elizabeth Tuke
COURTESY THE ARCHIVES OF THE RETREAT

Part Two
The Evolution of Quakerism, 1700-1800:
Period of Conservatism, Organization, and Quietism

Quietism: A Rationalization of Earlier Beliefs

As Howard Brinton states, 'The period of creation was followed by a period of conservatism. No religious movement has ever maintained the fire, energy, and power which accompanied its formative period. . . . If religion is to become a part of life itself, it must become integrated with the routine affairs of family living'.[45] Rufus Jones, a renowned Friend thinker, in his *Later Periods of Quakerism* writes of the changed intellectual climate and altered outlook one finds in Quakerism when passing from the 17th to the 18th century. He states, 'Spiritual movements, like life itself, are subjected to the shaping forces of an ever-shifting environment. They cannot go on unmodified'.[49] He further argues that 'the very tendency of habit which appears in all human undertakings would seem, *a priori*, to give continuity and fixity and permanence to a spiritual movement, but in reality the very formation of habit profoundly alters a movement and changes its character and quality as well as its intensity'.[50] Jones concludes that, 'The old words come to mean something different on the lips of a new generation'.[51] Habit, custom and discipline became the emphasis of 18th-century Quakers, in contrast to the creativity and fire so apparent at the 17th-century birth of the movement.

Because of this shift, the period from 1700-1800 often is referred to as the period of Quietism, but the traditional definition of 'quiet' does not apply. Quietism in the Quaker sense was the doctrine 'that every self-centered trait or activity must be suppressed or quieted in order that the divine may find unopposed entrance to the soul'.[52] Rufus Jones states that Quietism did not imply 'lethargy and inaction; it [did] not mean folded hands and a little more sleep. . . . The Quietests . . . often . . . [swung] out into a course of action that would make the rationally centered Christian quail with fear. . . '.[53] For 18th-century Quakers, the question was the 'right way to initiate action'. For them, thoughts that originated in man were 'spiritually barren', but when human motives were 'quieted', the 'divine' would spontaneously lead the way to correct behavior.[54] Following the Act of Toleration in the late 1600's, Quakers were weary from persecution. Howard Brinton states that 'Most of the first leaders had died, many of them in prison, and a second generation was coming on who were not motivated by the blinding fire and acute zeal that comes from the discovery of a new truth or from resistance to violent opposition.'[55] The Meeting emerged as the center for cultivating the notion of a 'quiet' following of inward guidance, and the Society became a 'well-ordered, highly integrated community of interdependent members'.[56]

Meeting for Worship: The Center of the 18th-century Quaker Community

In short, the 18th-century Quaker Meeting for Worship was less spectacular than the public professions of George Fox, but it was to become the enduring legacy of the Quaker movement.[57] The silent waiting or 'Quietism' cultivated in the Meeting found its roots in mysticism. Mysticism can be defined as a 'religious experience based on the spiritual search for an inward, immediate experience of the divine'.[58] In other words, Meetings for Worship were to be conducive to the inward search for the Light, but they were meant to be independent of outer forms and organization. Quaker worship wanted to prevent the substitution of form for spirit. This was because the

> religion and prophets of the Old Testament and the religion of the early Christian Church were based, not on form and tradition, but in the case of the prophets, on immediate experience of the voice of God in the soul, or, in the case of the early church, on the renewing and resurrecting power of the Christ Within.[59]

Meeting in the 18th century was 'an impressive exhibition of a Quietism that was corporate rather than individualistic'.[60] For almost every Member, there existed a

> deep-seated fear of everything 'man-made', and we see a variety of methods in operation designed to suppress 'own-self' and to hamper or crucify the 'creature'. Corporate silence – a silence prolonged unbroken sometimes for hours – came more and more as the century progressed, to be exalted as the loftiest way of worship. The silence of all flesh, the suppression of all strain and effort, the slowing down of all the mechanisms of action, the hushing of all the faculties of thought, were urged as the true preparation for receiving the divine word.[61]

In general, prayer within the Quaker Meeting was now silent and inwardly guided as opposed to the vocal fervor of the 17th century. However, the will and feelings of the worshiper might be sufficiently aroused 'that he must communicate to the Meeting what has come to him'.[62] Some within the Meeting in the 18th century even became acknowledged ministers who spoke as 'the mouthpiece of the group'.[63] Anyone was able to speak out and allegedly there was no discrimination against any sex, class, or age. As mentioned earlier, however, abundant Retreat records of women who spoke out in Meeting suggest that the rhetoric may not have matched the practice. The fact that anyone was allowed to speak out might also have created a situation inherently more likely to heighten sensitivity to the presence of someone who was troubled in mind. If there was a mentally ill person in the Meeting, the other Members quite probably became immediately aware of it through his or her outwardly confused verbal expression.

The same Light that provided for the primacy of individual experience also probably prompted the creation of the system of governance within the Society of Friends. Pure mysticism would have failed to foster such a method of union. The Religious Society of Friends separated itself from other religious groups of the period by developing a type of group mysticism grounded in Christian concepts.[64] With the formation of the Meeting community as an organic whole, united by the divine spirit, Quakers began to give structure to their movement. The truths articulated by George Fox became embodied in an organization, and they were able to be propagated by traveling ministers much in the way that the beliefs and concerns articulated by William Tuke were actualized in the formation of The Retreat and then propagated by those who wrote and talked about them.

It is not surprising that the tradition of the immediate experience of the Divine in a community atmosphere of silent waiting would lead to social reform. In contrast to the Catholic and Protestant churches, where spiritual exercises might be received passively, that which arose in a Quaker Meeting was the result of individually inspired activity. The pioneering quality of William Tuke's reforms was definitely due in part to the character of the Meeting for Worship in which silent waiting permitted

> a fresh and direct facing of facts under conditions in which the conscience [that measure of Light given each person] becomes sensitized. There is no screen of words between soul and reality. . . . the worshiper finds a certain condition in the outside world presented to his mind at the very time at which he is seeking God's guidance for his actions. The horizontal human relationship becomes correlated with the vertical divine relationship in such a way that certain actions appear to be required independently of any human opinion or demand. A concern develops and with it a sense of uneasiness over a situation about which something needs to be done. This uneasiness persists until the required action is undertaken either successfully or unsuccessfully.[65]

Elders and Overseers

A group of Quakers called Elders gradually evolved in a role of authority to guide those who spoke in Meeting. In 1765, they helped acknowledged ministers to discover divinely inspired words or thoughts of 'power and life'.[66] Eldering sought to place only that limitation on the individual that would still allow for the freedom of the group as a whole.[67] Quakerism at this time developed a distinctive cultural pattern, and the Elders helped enforce the Quaker beliefs in plain speech, plain dress, and plain behavior.

Elders attempted to identify and guard convention, and a group called the Overseers was established to guide conduct in two important ways. The Overseers visited those who fell short of the standards of Quaker behavior, and they issued Queries to be answered by local Meetings who might then compare their responses with the ideals of behavior set forth by the Religious Society of Friends generally. Quakerism, which had begun as a group in the time of George Fox and traditionally was held together by a bond of fellowship, now required an organizational structure to deal with the practical concerns of the various Meetings.

The strictness of the discipline of the Elders was evidenced in the patient case records of The Retreat. Many were disowned because of marriage outside of the Society, or they were judged to be immoral because of behavioral practices such as superfluity of dress or overconsumption.[68] Some of those who did not 'follow the rules' were likely labeled insane. Further, at least a few who did not 'meet the standard' may well have sought refuge at The Retreat. William Tuke himself became concerned about the poor state of discipline within the Society in the 18th century. He perceived that 'laxity, partiality, formality and perhaps spiritual pride had crept into its [the Meeting's] proceedings, and he often believed it his duty to oppose the course which the principal members were disposed to adopt'.[69]

Eighteenth-Century Meeting and The Retreat: Models of the Family

The Meeting that emerged as the center of the Quaker community was a synthesis of individuality and group life, much like that which develops within a family. The habits learned were carried by Quakers into the routine of their daily lives. The occupational therapy, tea parties, and the Appendage sited near The Retreat were all efforts to recreate a social situation at the asylum similar to that of a Meeting family in which positive habits might be learned. Like a Friends Meeting, The Retreat was a sheltered community that aimed at becoming a training ground for life on the 'outside'. For Quakers, both in the Meeting and at The Retreat, the most effective form of learning was by experience. The ability to follow the Inner Light was a 'learned' process which took place through inner discipline. Moral treatment in fact attempted to cure patients by instilling in them a sense of internal control. This process went below the level of ideas gained by formal teaching to the level of the will. The concept of an 'internalized locus of control' was of central interest, and it was thought to be the surest technique for curing insanity. Thought and action were to become integrated through experience – like learning science by involvement in the laboratory method rather than by simply hearing a lecture alone.[70]

In Meeting, no voting was ever conducted. Instead, decisions were reached by consensus with individual authority subservient to the authority

View of the North east Front of the proposed Asylum near Philadelphia

Friends Asylum, founded in 1813 near Philadelphia, Pennsylvania, was America's first private non-profit, psychiatric hospital, modelled closely on The York Retreat. It was established to provide humane care for 'persons deprived of the use of their reason'. The institution's name was changed to Friends Hospital in 1914.

of the group. It was believed that the whole Meeting could see more truth than a single person. There could be no supremacy of a majority over a minority. In fact, unlike voting, which brought forth no new possibilities, discussion of an issue in the search for consensus often created 'cross-fertilizations' and expansions of the original idea. In addition, a more radical minority might gradually convince the majority, a process which would not take place with just a simple vote. William Tuke, often himself in the minority, had the difficult task of convincing the majority of the necessity of establishing The Retreat. Through deliberation, he was able to convince other Friends of its necessity, reach the consensus to move ahead, and structure a planning committee.[71] Decisions by The Retreat committees were arrived at by consensus, but as mentioned earlier female staff did not participate in many of the deliberations.

The Quaker Meeting was not only analogous to a family by being a formative ground for spiritual and intellectual behavior, but it was also similar in that it provided economic support as well. In the 18th century, the Meeting became the means of financial sustenance for some of its Members. The persecution of Quakers was often accompanied by fines, and Friends were required to turn to one another for support. Members were economically interdependent, and the first list of Members of the Religious Society of Friends ever published was one which listed those entitled to fiscal assistance.[72] The Members' children were also named, and from this practice came the idea of a 'birthright Friend'. There was no state support for the poor or sick in the 17th or 18th centuries, and this substantial burden also became the responsibility of the Meeting.[73] The Meeting was then both 'a religious and economic unit' much 'like a large family whose members [were] dependent on one another, not only for material necessities, but for intellectual and spiritual well-being'.[74]

This notion of economic, intellectual, and spiritual interdependence was continued within the walls of The Retreat. The patients and staff were commonly referred to as the 'Family'. Many poor patients received economic support from other Quakers or through Subscriptions from Monthly Meetings because they could not afford the expense of The Retreat.[75] George and Catherine Jepson further built upon the notion of family as 'mother and father figure' superintendents. Jepson and Tuke each worked one year for free to contribute to the family, and the staff and patients were expected to cooperate like family members in chores around The Retreat.[76] In addition, letters from the families of patients assumed a particularly affectionate tone toward William Tuke and the other staff. They were written as if to very close relatives.[77]

Conclusion

The Quaker ideals of community, harmony, equality, and simplicity as developed through the first century and a half since its creation illuminate

Quakerism as a process which allowed and encouraged the establishment of The York Retreat. However, the rhetoric of Quakerism more than infrequently fell short in practice, and this was also reflected in moral treatment. The Retreat community mirrored the Quaker Meeting family in its economic, spiritual, and intellectual unity, especially as influenced by the shared Light Within. Harmony, as unity of action reached through consensus and without coercion, manifested itself through William Tuke's reasoned and consistent appeal to those who might differ with his ideas. Some methods of coercion were occasionally employed at The Retreat, however, such as secluding rooms and straitjackets. Perhaps pacifistic ideas periodically only 'sounded good', and when it came to 'management' of the mad resorting to coercion was sometimes judged appropriate.

Equality manifested itself through The Retreat's acceptance of patients regardless of their economic background. Women staff, however, were not treated as full equals in The Retreat's decision-making processes, and some women appear to have been labeled insane for speaking up in Meeting. Additionally, wealthy patients received better accommodations than those who came on subscription. Simplicity was expressed by the condemnation of superfluous activities and the exaltation of the practice of necessary daily activities. Patients were encouraged to partake in sewing, washing, and gardening, and they were discouraged from reading or art which were seen as representations of life that tended to take the place of life itself. Verbalism and formalism were opposed, and instead the study of 'practical' science books was encouraged.[78] Nevertheless, The Retreat's environment was anything but simple. Accommodations, gardens, meals, and beverages verged on the extravagant. Despite the inherent contradictions and intermittently flawed aspects of The Retreat, however, the most important feature was its vast improvement over other institutions. The evolution of Quakerism had provided the basis for the beginning of a more humane treatment of the insane.

It is like the story of the Chinese sage Lao-Tse, the founder of Taoism, who on his death bed asked his disciple to look into his mouth. ' "What do you see?" the old one asked. . . . "No teeth, but I see a tongue." By this Lao-Tse taught him this lesson: that which is hard, sharp and brittle disappears, while that which is soft and yielding survives.'[79] It may have taken a century and a half for George Fox's ideals to have become a reality, but the tongue of moral treatment permanently crushed the brittle teeth of 17th-century violent methods of dealing with the insane. The social, economic, and structural evolution of Quakerism, coupled with beliefs that were there from the beginning of the movement, were the indispensable elements that made it possible for the Society of Friends to be among the first to institute 'moral treatment' for the mentally ill.

Notes

[1] George Fox, *Epistles I Volume 7: The Works of George Fox* (New York: AMS Press, 1975), p. 343.

[2] Howard Brinton, *Friends for 300 Years* (Harper and Brothers, 1952; rpt. Wallingford, Pennsylvania: Pendle Hill Publishers, 1983), pp. 88-89.

[3] Hugh Barbour and J. William Frost, *The Quakers* (Connecticut: Greenwood Press, 1988), p. 5.

[4] BIHR, *Directors' Minute Book* 1792-1841, p. 4. Historians who have suggested the death of Hannah Mills as the explanation for the founding of The Retreat include: Samuel Tuke, *Description of The Retreat*, p. 22. Gregory Zilboorg, *Medical History of Psychology*, p. 572. William K. and E. Margaret Sessions, *The Tukes of York*, p. 58. Anne Digby, *Madness, Morality, and Medicine*, p. 12.

[5] See Mary Glover, *The Retreat, York*, pp. 11-14. William and Margaret Sessions, *The Tukes of York*, p. 67. Andrew Scull, *Madhouses, Mad-doctors, Madmen*, p. 110 (Scull is more concerned with the social roots of the practice of moral treatment itself). Anne Digby, *Madness, Morality, and Medicine*, p. 28-29. Michel Foucault in *Madness and Civilization* presents a flawed argument by failing to address the motivations for founding The Retreat and instead focusing only on the practice once it was established.

[6] William and Margaret Sessions, *The Tukes of York* (York, England: William Sessions Limited: The Ebor Press, 1971), p. 1. William Tuke's grandfather was in fact imprisoned twice in York in the 1660's for his Quaker beliefs.

[7] Howard Brinton, *Friends for 300 Years*, pp. 175-202.

[8] Mircea Eliade, *Encyclopedia of Religion*, Vol. 12 (New York: Macmillan, 1987), p. 130.

[9] Howard Brinton, *Friends for 300 Years*, p. 16.

[10] Hugh Barbour and J. William Frost, *The Quakers*, p. 4.

[11] Howard Brinton, *Friends for 300 Years*, p. 7.

[12] Anne Harrington, Lecture on Moral Treatment, History of Science 175, October, 1989.

[13] William and Margaret Sessions, *The Tukes of York*, p. 55.

[14] Howard Brinton, *Friends for 300 Years*, p. 85.

[15] Philadelphia Yearly Meeting, *Faith and Practice* (Philadelphia Yearly Meeting of the Religious Society of Friends, 1972), pp. 1-2.

[16] *Faith and Practice*, p. 56. Also, see section on 'Spiritual Experiences of Friends'.

[17] Hugh Barbour and J. William Frost, *The Quakers*, p. 27.

[18] Elizabeth Isichei, *Victorian Quakers* (London: Oxford University Press, 1970), p. 6.

[19] Howard Brinton, *Friends for 300 Years*, p. 3.

[20] Howard Brinton, p. 4.

[21] William and Margaret Sessions, *The Tukes of York*, p. 55.

[22] William and Margaret Sessions, p. 67.

[23] Howard Brinton, *Friends for 300 Years*, p. 64.

[24] Howard Brinton, p. 64.

[25] Howard Brinton, p. 64.

[26] Howard Brinton, p. 28.

[27] Howard Brinton, p. 44.

[28] Hugh Barbour and J. William Frost, *The Quakers*, p. 62.

29 Howard Brinton, *Friends for 300 Years*, p.45.
30 Hugh Barbour and J. William Frost, *The Quakers*, p.63.
31 Hugh Barbour and J. William Frost, p.63.
32 Howard Brinton, *Friends for 300 Years*, pp.44-48.
33 Howard Brinton, p.210.
34 *Faith and Practice*, pp.2-3.
35 Barry Reay, *The Quakers and the English Revolution* (London: Maurice Temple Smith Ltd., 1985), p.106.
36 Howard Brinton, *Friends for 300 Years*, p.101.
37 Howard Brinton, p.151.
38 William and Margaret Sessions, *The Tukes of York*, p.1.
39 Howard Brinton, *Friends for 300 Years*, p.158.
40 Arthur Raistrick, *Quakers in Science and Industry* (New York: Philosophical Library, 1950), p.36.
41 William and Margaret Sessions, *The Tukes of York*, p.1.
42 Howard Brinton, *Friends for 300 Years*, p.138.
43 Arthur Raistrick, *Quakers in Science and Industry*, p.44.
44 Arthur Raistrick, p.44 & pp.319-333.
45 From a conversation with Dr Alistair Gordon, Superintendent of The Retreat from 1979 to the present, while visiting The York Retreat, August, 1989.
46 William and Margaret Sessions, *The Tukes of York*, p.22.
47 BIHR, The Retreat Archives.
48 Howard Brinton, *Friends for 300 Years*, p.181.
49 Rufus Jones, *Later Periods of Quakerism* (London: Macmillan and Co., 1921), p.32.
50 Rufus Jones, p.32.
51 Rufus Jones, p.33.
52 Howard Brinton, *Friends for 300 Years*, p.66.
53 Rufus Jones, *Later Periods of Quakerism*, p.35.
54 Rufus Jones, p.36.
55 Howard Brinton, *Friends for 300 Years*, p.182.
56 Howard Brinton, p.184.
57 For an interesting case study of the organization and development of Quaker meetings from the time of George Fox to the early 1800's see *Early Friends in the North* by John W. Steel.
58 Howard Brinton, *Friends for 300 Years*, p.xii.
59 Howard Brinton, p.17.
60 Rufus Jones, *Later Periods of Quakerism*, p.62.
61 Rufus Jones, p.63.
62 Howard Brinton, *Friends for 300 Years*, p.75.
63 Howard Brinton, p.84.
64 Howard Brinton, p.xiii.
65 Howard Brinton, p.145.
66 Howard Brinton, p.93.
67 Howard Brinton, p.93.
68 BIHR, Case Books.
69 William and Margaret Sessions, *The Tukes of York*, p.12.
70 Howard Brinton uses the scientific laboratory method as an analogy for the Quaker integration of thought and action in his book *Friends for 300 Years*.
71 BIHR, Directors' Minute Book, p.14.

[72] Rufus Jones, *Later Periods of Quakerism*, p.108.
[73] Howard Brinton, *Friends for 300 Years*, p.126.
[74] Howard Brinton, pp.126-127.
[75] BIHR, Committee Reports.
[76] BIHR, Case Books.
[77] BIHR, Correspondence, 1796-1812.
[78] Samuel Tuke, *Description of The Retreat*, p.183.
[79] Howard Brinton, *Friends for 300 Years*, p.165.

'Finally, dear friends, we affectionately intreat you, who have been sincerely concerned to follow Christ in the regeneration, whereby ye have been enabled to walk as good examples to others, hold fast that which you have, and still press forward, with a single eye to the Spirit of truth, that nothing may be suffered to prevent your attainment of that blessed promise "To him that overcometh will I give to eat of the tree of life, which is in the midst of the paradise of God"!

'The grace of our Lord Jesus Christ be with you all. Amen.

Signed in and on behalf of the said meeting by

Clerk to the Meeting this year.'

The Epistle to Friends at Yearly Meeting 1783, signed by William Tuke as Clerk.

CHAPTER FOUR

Conclusion: Integration of Historiography, Archival Material, and the Evolution of Quakerism

THIS ESSAY HAS NOT BEEN A chronological narrative or a neatly laid argument in which each point builds upon the previous one. Instead, a common object – the nature of the asylum reform represented by The York Retreat – has been examined through a variety of lenses. Chapter One juxtaposed the historiographic perspectives of writers ranging from Samuel Tuke in 1813 to Anne Digby in 1985, showing the astonishing dissonances of opinion – especially between those individuals I have called 'insiders' and those I have called 'outsiders' – that exist in the literature on the historical 'meaning' of the York reforms. Attention was paid in particular to certain of the author's ideological biases which may have led them to neglect or distort certain dimensions of The Retreat story, or to focus on the data that they did. In Chapter Two, a re-examination of the archival material allowed questions and objections to be raised about at least certain aspects of the standing historical interpretations. Chapter Three provided an historical introduction to those aspects of Quakerism critical to understanding the founding of The Retreat as well as the philosophy behind its practice once it opened; lack of such an analysis was, it can be argued, a common problem with virtually all accounts of The Retreat offered by historians to date.

This final chapter attempts to bring the various elements of the essay into one converging image by inviting the reader to see what the historical problem of asylum reform 'looks like' when the different windows that have been offered into it are laid side by side:

Issue 1: Impetus behind the founding of The Retreat

Historical Perspectives	*Archival Perspectives*	*Historical Perspectives on Quakerism*
Tuke, the Sessions, Zilboorg, Digby–The Retreat as a reaction to Hannah Mills' death	Hannah Mills' death relatively trivial to the story	Humane care for the insane and asylum reform advocated as early as George Fox's time
Glover, Scull, Digby– The Retreat as part of shift in world view; madman now seen as human instead of animal		Reform delayed until late 18th century for economic and political reasons
Zilboorg–The Retreat as a result of the State's interest in the destitute		Quaker Retreat an independent venture; Quakers oppressed by State

Issue 2: Quaker versus non-Quaker nature of The Retreat

Historical Perspectives	*Archival Perspectives*	*Historical Perspectives on Quakerism*
Tuke–The Retreat for protection of Quaker patients from non-Quaker patients and staff	Admission of non-Quaker patients from 1796	Quakers suffered fines, were imprisoned and became protectionist
Tuke–The Retreat for patients not strictly Members of Society; subscriptions accepted from non-Quakers	Subscriptions from non-Members Government only by Quakers Preference for Quaker staff	Quakers of late 18th century became separatist through self-defined rules and social networks. This led to at least partial isolation from bourgeois
Foucault–The Retreat as instrument of religious segregation		
Scull–The Retreat recreated an isolated bourgeois society		
Godlee–The Retreat initially run by Quakers for Quakers		
Digby–Non-Quakers admitted 1820		

Issue 3: Women at The Retreat

Historical Perspectives	*Archival Perspectives*	*Historical Perspectives on Quakerism*
Digby–Women staff respected as much as men	Women as integral part of 'father/mother' superintendent teams	Discrepancy between rhetoric and practice; women were equals according to Quaker beliefs, but in reality
Tuke–Refers to Female Visitors only in footnote	Women not included in decisions concerning	

Historical Perspectives	*Archival Perspectives*	*Historical Perspectives on Quakerism*
Foucault–Women as insignificant part of patriarchal hierarchy	government of The Retreat Female Visitors' suggestions only followed if approved by all-male committee	were not encouraged to participate in the committee sessions for the government of Monthly Meetings

Issue 4: Integration of medical and moral treatment

Historical Perspectives	*Archival Perspectives*	*Historical Perspectives on Quakerism*
Digby–Admissions based on Quaker versus non-Quaker background of patient, not medical diagnosis Digby–Cure by divine intervention Tuke, Zilboorg, Glover, the Sessions– Cure through diet, fresh air, exercise, etc.	Heroic treatments employed Medical certificates required for admission 'Incurables' generally turned away Biological as well as moral causes of insanity	Science supported by Quaker beliefs; human perfectibility, righteousness by works, mind/body unity

Issue 5: Moral Treatment: control or cure?

Historical Perspectives	*Archival Perspectives*	*Historical Perspectives on Quakerism*
Foucault–Patients controlled by system of rewards and punishments; guilt-producing Scull–Patients reshaped into bourgeois ideal of individual Digby–Patients as school children to be reeducated Godlee–Patients forced to conform to Quaker norms	Permissive atmosphere seemed to reign in some instances; patients and families decided length of patient stay Records of suicides, restraint methods, secluding room, and class distinctions	Quaker doctrine of the 'Inner Light' saw self-discipline as a liberating quality that allowed an individual to follow his/her own divine leadings Shift from religious movement to sect required imposing conformism on Members

What can be said about these observations? This brief chapter will argue that column three of the above chart – historical perspectives on Quakerism – is, in many cases, in a position to mediate between and/or account for tensions among historiographical accounts on the one hand, and archival data on the other. This last section will not analyze piece-for-piece the items on the table, but will instead focus on two critical issues which have defined the parameters of the debate about moral treatment since the time of Samuel Tuke:

(1) Was moral treatment both a reaction against and a rejection of medical treatment?
(2) Was the effect of moral treatment humane and liberating or guilt-inducing?

Historians such as Samuel Tuke, Mary Glover, Gregory Zilboorg, and the Sessions have suggested that The Retreat's practices represented a radical rejection of traditional medical techniques. In the place of heroic methods a system of 'moral treatment', emphasizing occupational therapy, talking, diet, fresh air, and exercise, was employed. William Bynum, in his article 'Rationales for Therapy in British Psychiatry, 1780-1835', argues that one reason for this abandonment of medical methods was that in the 18th century, 'Their universe was more nearly Cartesian than ours in . . . separation of mind from brain. . . . How in a Cartesian universe, can physicians cure mental diseases by physical remedies?'[1] He continues to observe that the 'growing medical interest in and control over the insane was . . . challenged by the spread of moral therapy . . . [which suggests that] that which is psychologically caused is most effectively psychologically treated'.[2] Further, 'if laymen like the Tukes could operate a more effective asylum than doctors . . . traditional therapeutic regimes and theories of insanity were both jeopardized'.[3]

Was the threat of The Retreat and moral therapy to the medical control of the insane actually as dramatic as Bynum states? The archival data and the history of Quakerism suggest not. As mentioned previously, medical methods were not discarded at The Retreat, and, in fact, The Retreat doctors employed virtually all of the traditional heroic medical techniques including leeches, purges, and emetics. An understanding of this seemingly puzzling fact can begin to be reached when we consider that Quakers were not 'Cartesian' in their philosophy about the mind and body, and they would have had no metaphysical reasons upon which to reject medical therapeutics (with the exception that they rejected some traditional methods because of the experimental discovery that they basically did not work).

For Quakers, every person was an indivisible whole of mind (soul) and body, which would have allowed for treatment of the insane through medicine and faith, sympathy and science. Taking this argument still further, Quaker beliefs may actually have supported the development of science, including medical science, in a fashion reminiscent of the way in which the Puritan system of ethics was conducive to the rise of scientific values in 17th-century England.[4] Quakers believed in the possibility of human perfectibility. There was a 'partnership' of the material and the spiritual, and a regard for what they called the 'doctrine of continuing revelation'. For Quakers, the world was in a process of constant change, and there was no final, complete, absolute truth. Friends believed that individuals looked to God for guidance, but that was not enough. Once spiritually enlightened, man had to play an active role in improving life for himself and others.

Another central issue in the debate about moral treatment concerns the nature of the method itself. As previously discussed, some historians have followed in the tradition of Foucault by calling The Retreat's therapy a 'moral imprisonment', a 'mechanism of conformity', a 'guilt-producing' environment, and a 're-creation of the bourgeois society'. Whiggish historians, on the other hand, have considered moral treatment the essential gift of freedom for the madman.

The history of Quakerism provides a framework for seeing how The York Retreat may have been, in fact, interested both in control and cure, rather than in either one or the other. In the 18th century, there was an increased emphasis in the Quaker community on controlling the behavior of Members. Elders and Overseers visited those who did not live up to the expected standards, and some Friends were disowned for not obeying 'the rules'. This push toward conformism was reflected in the practice at The Retreat. Quakers, however, still held a strong belief in the Inner Light as a liberating principle. Every individual had 'that of God' within, and a realization of his strength was the first step toward his re-integration into society where self-control was required.

Notes

[1] William Bynum, 'Rationales for Therapy in British Psychiatry, 1780-1835' in *Madhouses, Mad-doctors, Madmen* (Philadelphia: The University of Pennsylvania Press, 1981), pp.38-39.

[2] William Bynum, pp.41-42.

[3] William Bynum, p.46.

[4] Robert K. Merton, *Science, Technology, and Society in Seventeenth Century England* (Belgium: St Catherine Press, 1936). Steven Harris' 'Transposing the Merton Thesis: Apostolic Spirituality and the Establishment of the Jesuit Scientifc Tradition' (forthcoming in *Science in Context*) offers a similar account of the Society of Jesus' support of the rise of science.

Afterword

AN ESSENTIAL TENET OF THE QUAKER FAITH is that there is no 'final truth'. As a Friend, an awareness of the necessary limits on the human ability to reach absolute answers has given me a framework for coming to terms with the complexities of the many 'truths' contained in the varying historiographic accounts of The York Retreat. My own perspective on this dialogue has been informed, on the one hand, by an unwillingness to indulge in hagiography and, on the other, by a reluctance to capitulate to the 'conspiracy theory' of the sociologically-oriented historians since Foucault. It is not just that I have sought to mediate a middle ground at any price. Rather, my training both as a Friend and as a student of the history of science has coalesced in a fruitful way to convince me that one simply sees more clearly by standing in the middle of the road. This skepticism toward extremes in either direction could be seen as a quintessentially Quaker rejection of the 'either/or' for the 'both/and'. In this thesis I have sought not to arrest the pendulum of historiographical debate, but to steady its violence in the service of greater historical and human clarity.

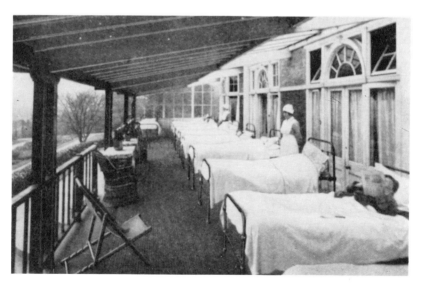

Open-Air Treatment at The York Retreat, 1932.

Appendix

THE FOLLOWING IS AN EXACT TRANSCRIPTION of the actual notes recorded in the *First Visitors Book*. Spellings have been kept in accordance with the practice of the time. The book includes descriptions of the visitors to The Retreat, and casts doubt on the claim that The Retreat was isolated from larger society.

First Visitors Book D/3/1A

1811 3 mo. Lewis Simond, a Frenchman, wrote, 'Travels of a frenchman through Britain,' a second edition is come out since – Sydney Smith came with him.
1798 2 27 The Earl of Warwick's Brother expressed his approbation in strong terms.
   Dr. De la Reve from Geneva & Dr. Turner from Cambridge. The former travelling in quest of information in favour of an Institution for Lunatics going to be established in Swisserland – he was very inquisitive & both expressed much satisfaction.
   6 29 Dr. Duncan of Edinburgh and Dr. Albers, a German Physician.
1799 1 mo. A Gentleman from Russia of the name of Deriabin who has travelled over most parts of Europe and America with a view of gaining information respecting charitable Institutions & promoting similar ones for the good of his country. Dr. Cappe accompanied him.
1798 10 28 Deriabin, an officer in the Russian army
1799 11 18 Sr. Robt. Hillyard, Col. Stourbenzie, Col. Crow, Capt. Gail, Capt. Lieutenant Smelt.
1803 3 mo. 11th Abrm. Barker, New Bedford, Massachusetts. N. America, a young man (a Friend) on a tour; has been in Russia, Denmark, Sweden & Holland.
   8 10 Dr. Hooper, Tooley Strees, London with his Wife, Daughter, & Sister. His sister, an agreeable unassuming young woman, left in a Note sealed up £50, with a request that her name not appear in the accounts
1814 3 2 G. Home Summer N. P., St. Georges Street, Wesminster, London – Lindley (& Wood) Architects, Doncaster
   C. A. Burby, 33, Bowers Street, London, Archt.
   Dr. Olive of Dublin
   Dr. Freer, a professor, Glasgow College
1814 8 mo. 13 Dr. Hamel of St. Petersburg, Physician to the Emporer, M^r. de Leval, Chamberlain to H. I. M. the emporer of all the Russias, & a princess of Russia

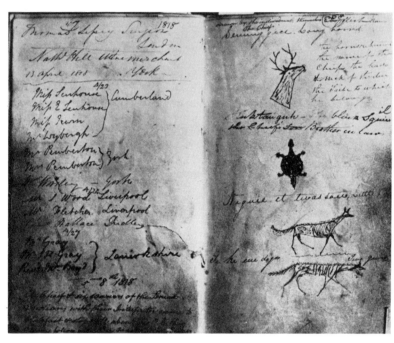

Two pages from the Visitors' Book *(including entries made by Indian Warriors)*
COURTESY ARCHIVES OF THE THE RETREAT, YORK

9 30 Robt. Paget, Exmouth, Devon, Thomas H. Burder, Camberwell Grove nr. London, two young men students at Edin.

12 1 Dr. Henderson, London, has been lately at Paris. He dined with Dr. Pinel & viewed the Asylum he attends

1815 3 25 – Gregson from Liverpool

4 11 – Rutherford. a Councillor of Law, a Gent.^{n} from Edinburgh

5 6 Robt. Owen from Lanark, Scotland. He remarked that on visiting houses of this kind his feelings had been harrowed esp., but at this house he was not so affected

19 Baron de Hahn, Officer in the service of the H. I. M. the Emporer of all the Russias.

5 mo. 15 – Sam.l Waring Jr. Bridgewater, Somerset

1815 6 mo. 30 Charles Duncombe Esq. Dunscombe Park. M. P. Dr. Weire, Inspector of Naval Hospitals – Admiralty, &

7 1 Edw'd Hall, No. 7 Great Cheyne Row, Chelsea, or Surveyor of Buildings Navy Office

7 30 Robt. Longdon from Derby, a young man Igna Arch.t Durham

Mrs. Jennings – York

Miss Jennings – York

Sam.l Bottomley Jr. Scarbro.

10 21 Sir William Rae Edinburgh

Lady Rae

Miss Champs of Elvington

10 23 Two sisters of the name of Humphrey from London Asylum (with Jno. Mason)

10 mo. 26th Sam.l Bradshaw, York. Retired & his wife

11 5 Chas. Price, Jr. London – a Governor of Bethlem. Hospl.

Son of Jn. Chs. Price from Dublin

11 10 Miss Warrens – York

Miss Laycock – York

John Wm. Francis, M.D. of N. York

J. W. Francis is not wholly ignorant of the state of the Lunatic Asylum in North America, and he visited almost all the institutions for the Insane that are established in England. He now embraces this opportunity of stating that after an examination of The Retreat for some hours, he should do injustice to his feelings were he not to declare that this establishment far surpasses anything he has elsewhere seen, and that it reflects equal credit on the wisdom and humanity of its conductors. Perhaps it is no inconsiderable honour to add that Institutions of a similar nature and on this same plan are organising in different parts of the United States. The New world cannot do better than imitate the Old so far as concerns the management of those who labour under mental infirmities.

Nov. 30, 1815

J.W.F.
New York

Bibliography

Archival Sources

The archives for The York Retreat are located at the Borthwick Institute for Historical Research in York, England. The records are well-preserved and, according to the archivists, 'little has been discarded'. Archival documents are labeled according to a letter and number system. The letter represents a category heading and the number indicates the particular box for the document. The material used in this paper consists of records from the first two decades of The Retreat's proposed founding and actual functioning (1792-1812) under the following subdivisions:

Administrative Records
    Directors' Minute Books A/1/1
    Directors' Rough Minute Books A/2/1
    Committee Minute Books B/3/1A

Correspondence and Papers
    General Correspondence (letters) C/1/1

Visitors' Records
    Visitors' Books D/3/1A

Financial Records
    Subscription Books E/1/1
    Subscriptions and Handbills about The Retreat 1793-1796 E/2
    General Ledgers E/3/1 and E/3/2 and E/3/3
    General Cash Books E/4/1 and E/4/2 and E/4/3

The Retreat Building
    Building Accounts and Papers H/1/1

Admissions Records
    Returns of Admission J/2
    Register of Patients J/3/2

Medical Records
    Registers of Certificates K/1/1
    Case Books K/2/1 and K/2/1A

Miscellania
    Historical Notes by H. C. Hunt L/1/3

Published Sources

Quaker History

There are, at present, no critical histories of the development of Quakerism in late 17th and early 18th-century England. That is, most analyses of Quaker beliefs in this time period are written by Friends and tend to be particularly celebratory. Because of the nature of these accounts, published sources were supplemented by an interview with Jerry Frost, an internationally known Quaker historian and Professor of Religion at Swarthmore College. Particularly helpful for an initial orientation in the history of the Friends movement was Howard Brinton's *Friends for Three Hundred Years*. Jerry Frost and Hugh Barbour offer an examination of American Quakerism in *The Quakers* with a helpful introduction on the founding of the Religious Society of Friends in England. The best sources for a description of Quaker beliefs and practice in the 18th century are Rufus Jones' *Later Periods of Quakerism*, Arnold Lloyd's *Quaker Social History*, and Elizabeth Isichei's *Victorian Quakers*. Arthur Raistrick, although not including a description of the role of Quakers in asylum reform, provides an interesting account of the history of Friends involvement in science in *Quakers in Science and Industry*. The symbol * indicates that the work is not found in the Harvard library system.

Barbour, Hugh and Frost, J. William. *The Quakers*. Connecticut: The Greenwood Press, 1988. W- BX 7731. 2. B37.

Brinton, Howard. *Friends for Three Hundred Years*. Wallingford, Pennsylvania: Pendle Hill Publications, 1952. AH BX 7631. B7.

Clark, Robert A., and J. Russell Elkinton. *The Quaker Heritage in Medicine*. Pacific Grove, California: The Boxwood Press, 1978. Me- BX 7747. C594q.

Frost, J. William. Professor of Religion, Swarthmore College. Interview, December 1989.

Grubb, Edward. *The Evangelical Movement*. Leominster: The Orphans' Printing Press, 1924. W- C 8310. 330.

Isichei, Elizabeth. *Victorian Quakers*. London: Oxford University Press, 1970. AH- C 8310. 540.

Jones, Rufus. *Later Periods of Quakerism*. London: Macmillan and Co., Limited, 1921. AH- BX 7631. J6.

Lloyd, Arnold. *Quaker Social History*. London: Longmans, Green and Co., 1950. H- C 8310. 535.

Philadelphia Yearly Meeting of the Religious Society of Friends. *Faith and Practice*. Philadelphia: Philadelphia Yearly Meeting, 1984.* (Faith and Practice of the New England Yearly Meeting can be found in the Andover-Harvard Theological Library AH- BX 7607. N4 A5.)

Raistrick, Arthur. *Quakers in Science and Industry*. New York: The Philosophical Library, Inc., 1950. AH- BX 7676. R3.

Reay, Barry. *The Quakers and the English Revolution.* London: Maurice
Temple Smith, 1985. AH- BX 7676. 2. R4.
Steel, John W. *Early Friends in the North.* London: Headley Brothers,
1905. W- C 8312. 350.

General History of Psychiatry

For an introduction to the history of psychiatry and asylum reform,
Richard Hunter and Ida Macalpine's book, *Three Hundred Years of
Psychiatry,* was particularly helpful. Andrew Scull's book, *Madhouses,
Mad-doctors, Madmen,* provided an invaluable collection of essays on
British psychiatry in the late 17th and early 18th centuries. Among this
collection, William Bynum's article, 'Rationales for Therapy in British
Psychiatry, 1780-1835', discussed the important tensions between medical
and moral therapy. *The Anatomy of Madness: Essays in the History of
Psychiatry,* edited by William F. Bynum et. al., included articles such as
Fiona Godlee's 'Aspects of non-conformity: Quakers and the lunatic fringe'
as well as a summary by Anne Digby of her larger work, *Madness, Morality,
and Medicine.* Elaine Showalter's work, *The Female Malady,* provided a
feminist analysis of the relation of women to mental illness from the 18th to
the 20th centuries in England. *Science, Technology, and Society in
Seventeenth Century England* by Robert K. Merton gives an account of
Puritanism and the rise of science which suggests a parallel model for
Quaker support of medical therapies. The symbol ★ indicates that the work
is not found in the Harvard library system.

Beers, Clifford. *A Mind That Found Itself.* New York: Longmans, Green,
1917. H- 157. B42.
Bucknill, John Charles, and Tuke, Daniel Hack. *Manual of Psychological
Medicine.* London: John Churchill, 1858. Me- WM 100 B925m.
Bynum, William F. et. al. *The Anatomy of Madness: Essays in the History
of Psychiatry.* London: Tavistock Publishing Company, 1985.
W- RC 450. A1 A53.
Bynum, William F. 'Rationales for Therapy in British Psychiatry, 1780-
1835' in *Madhouses, Mad-doctors, Madmen.* London: Allan Lane,
1979. W- RC 450. G7 S29.
Clare, Anthony. 'A Divided View of Madness' in *The Guardian,* London,
25 August, 1969, p.21. W- periodical room.
Digby, Anne. *From York Lunatic Asylum to Bootham Park Hospital.* York:
Borthwick Paper, 1986. W- DA 670. Y59 B6 no. 69.
Harrington, Anne. Assistant Professor of the History of Science, Harvard
University. Lecture, History of Science 175, October, 1989.
Merton, Robert K. *Science, Technology and Society in Seventeenth Century
England.* Bruges, Belgium: St Catherine Press, 1938.
W- Q127. G7 M45 x.

Roby, David S. *Pioneer of Moral Treatment: Isaac Bonsall & the Early Years of Friends Asylum as Recorded in Bonsall's Diaries 1817-1823.* Philadelphia: Winchell Company, 1982.★

Sanoff, Allan P. 'Sights Sacred and Profane.' *U.S. News and World Report*, 14 August, 1989, p.52. W- periodical room.

Scull, Andrew, ed. *Madhouses, Mad-doctors, Madmen: The Social History of Psychiatry in the Victorian Era.* Philadelphia: The University of Pennsylvania Press, 1981. W- RC450. G7 M26 X.

Scull, Andrew. *Museums of Madness: The Social Organization of Insanity in Nineteenth Century England.* London: Allan Lane, 1979. W- RC 450. G7 S29.

Showalter, Elaine. *The Female Malady.* New York: Pantheon Books, 1985. W- RC 451. 4. W6 S56.

Van Atta, Kim. *An Account of the Events Surrounding the Origin of Friends Hospital & A Brief Description of the Early Years of Friends Asylum 1817-1820.* Philadelphia: Winchell Company, 1980.★

The Retreat Histories

The following sources collectively represent the standing historical perspectives on the nature of The York Retreat asylum reform. The 'insiders', as defined in the thesis, are Samuel Tuke, Gregory Zilboorg, Mary Glover, and the Sessions; 'outsiders' perspectives are offered by Michel Foucault, Andrew Scull, Fiona Godlee, and Anne Digby. Of the previous authors, Anne Digby offers the most comprehensive account of the daily practices at The Retreat in her book *Madness, Morality, and Medicine*. Samuel Tuke's *Description of The Retreat* was the first full-length account of a mental hospital anywhere. The interview with Charles Cherry provided helpful background on the types of records kept in The Retreat archives. The symbol ★ indicates that the work is not found in the Harvard library system.

Cherry, Charles L. Professor of English and Associate Academic Vice President, Villanova University. Interview, July, 1989. Charles Cherry's book on The York Retreat and Friends Hospital, *A Quiet Haven: Quakers, Moral Treatment and Asylum Reform.* Fairleigh Dickinson University Press, Rutherford, New Jersey, 1989.

Committee of Management and Medical Director for The York Retreat. *The Retreat York Annual Report 1988.* York: William Sessions Limited, The Ebor Press, 1989.★

Digby, Anne. *Madness, Morality, and Medicine: A Study of The York Retreat, 1796-1914.* Cambridge: Cambridge University Press, 1985. Me- WM 28 FE5 D5Y.

Foucault, Michel. *Madness and Civilization: A History of Insanity in the Age of Reason*. New York: Random House, 1988. L-RC 438. F613.

Glover, Mary. *The Retreat, York: An Early Quaker Experiment in the Treatment of Mental Illness*. York: William Sessions Limited, 1984. W- RC 450. G72 Y674.

Godlee, Fiona. 'Aspects of non-conformity: Quakers and the lunatic fringe' in *The Anatomy of Madness: Essays in the History of Psychiatry*. London: Tavistock Publishing Company, 1985. W- RC 450. A1 A53.

Review of the Early History of The Retreat, York. York: Printed by John L. Linney, 1846.*

Sessions, William K. and E. Margaret. *The Tukes of York in the Seventeenth, Eighteenth, and Nineteenth Centuries*. York: William Sessions Limited, The Ebor Press, 1971. AH- CS439. T86.

A Sketch of the Origin, Progress, and Present State of The Retreat. York: Alexander and Son, Castlegate, 1828.*

Thurnam, John. *Statistics of The Retreat, near York 1796-1840*. York: Printed by John L. Linney, 1841.* (Available at Widener by the same author: *Observations and Essays on the Statistics of Insanity*. New York: Arno Press, 1976.) W- RC 340. T48.

Tuke, Samuel. *Description of The Retreat*. 1813; rpt. London: Dawsons of Pall Mall, 1964. Me- RC 450. E3. T81.

Zilboorg, Gregory. *A History of Medical Psychology*. New York: W. W. Norton & Company, 1941. H- 616. 8 Z69.

Reference Books

R. D. Conner's book *The Weights and Measures of England* was available at the Borthwick Institute, and provided information on historical British measurements which was invaluable in translating the medical records found in the archives. The *Encyclopedia of Religion* by Eliade Mircea was used as a reference for finding works on the history of Quakerism.

Conner, R. D. *The Weights and Measures of England*. London: Published by Her Majesty's Stationery Office and Trustees of the Science Museum, 1987. W- QC 89. G82 E543.

Eliade, Mircea, ed. *Encyclopedia of Religion*, Volume 12. New York: Macmillan, 1987. H- BL 31. E46.

Aerial view of The Retreat, York, 1989.
COURTESY THE RETREAT, YORK

SESSIONS OF YORK
ENGLAND